Christians believe traditional marriage matters because it is outlined for us in the pages of sacred Scripture. But guess what? Science, reason, and history are also on our side. In this excellent book, my friend Glenn Stanton explains how all of these roads point to the importance of marriage.

—JIM DALY, president, Focus on the Family

Cohabitation is growing in popularity across the United States as a way for couples to enjoy ready access to sex, to test drive their relationship, and even to have children together. Despite its current popularity, *The Ring Makes All the Difference* tells us two hard truths: cohabitation puts adults at risk for marital failure and children at risk of being exposed to a relational merry-go-round that all too often ends in neglect or abuse.

—W. BRADFORD WILCOX, director of National Marriage Project at the University of Virginia

This is an engaging and highly readable book describing why the ring matters. Glenn Stanton explains why marriage is different from other relationships like cohabitation, and how marriage benefits adults and children by signifying clarity about the nature of the commitment between two partners. It is both an important and a useful book.

—SCOTT M. STANLEY, research professor, University of Denver, author, *The Power of Commitment*

LOVED this book! An easy and insightful must-read for anybody thinking about living together or getting married as well as those working with young couples as pastors, counselors, or mentors.

—JULIE BAUMGARDNER, president and executive director of First Things First

THE RING MAKES ALL THE DIFFERENCE

The Hidden Consequences
of Cohabitation and the
Strong Benefits of Marriage

GLENN T. STANTON

MOODY PUBLISHERS
CHICAGO

All Scripture quotations, unless otherwise indicated, are taken from the *Holy Bible: New International Version*®. NIV®. Copyright ©1973, 1978, 1984 by Biblica, Inc. Used by permission of Zondervan. All rights reserved worldwide.

Websites and phone numbers listed herein are accurate at the time of publication, but may change in the future or cease to exist. The listing of website references and resources does not imply publisher endorsement of the sites' contents. Groups, corporations, and organizations are listed for informational purposes, and listing does not imply publisher endorsement of their activities.

Names have been changed to protect privacy.

Edited by Andy Scheer
Interior design: Ragont Design
Cover design: Maralynn Rochat
Cover images: Shadowed Ring: 3D Model, Maralynn Rochat

Library of Congress Cataloging-in-Publication Data

Stanton, Glenn T.
     The ring makes all the difference : the hidden consequences of cohabitation—and the strong benefits of marriage / Glenn T. Stanton.
       p. cm.
     Includes bibliographical references.
     ISBN 978-0-8024-0216-5
     1. Unmarried couples. 2. Unmarried couples—Religious aspects—Christianity.
     3. Marriage. 4. Marriage—Religious aspects—Christianity. I. Title.
HQ803.5.S73 2011
306.84'1—dc22

                                                                                    2011015751

We hope you enjoy this book from Moody Publishers. Our goal is to provide high-quality, thought-provoking books and products that connect truth to your real needs and challenges. For more information on other books and products written and produced from a biblical perspective, go to www.moodypublishers.com or write to:

Moody Publishers
820 N. LaSalle Boulevard
Chicago, IL 60610

1 3 5 7 9 10 8 6 4 2

Printed in the United States of America

Affectionately dedicated to my brother Todd,
his remarkable wife, Leslie,
and
their beautiful kids, Joshua and Lauren.

They allowed me to cohabit with them
at their home in Florida
during an enjoyable, monthlong writing sabbatical
to write this book.

Thank you, guys!

CONTENTS

WHEN we see the statistics,

we are scared witless at the possibility

of failing at what we want so badly:

marriage. So it makes it hard

for us to make the plunge.

COHABITATION NATION

Come live with me and be my love,
And we will some new pleasures prove
Of golden sands and crystal brooks
With silken line, and silver hooks
There's nothing that I wouldn't do
If you would be my POSSLQ.

You live with me, and I with you,
And you will be my POSSLQ.
I'll be your friend and so much more;
That's what a POSSLQ is for.

And everything we will confess;
Yes, even to the IRS.
Some day on what we both may earn,
Perhaps we'll file a joint return.
You'll share my pad, my taxes, joint.
You'll share my life, up to a point!
And that you'll be so glad to do,
Because you'll be my POSSLQ.[1]

COULD YOU BE A POSSLQ?

A S A NEW FORM OF SEXUAL and domestic relationship started to take hold in Western cultures in the 1970s, the US Census Bureau coined a new term—POSSLQ (pronounced *poss-el-cue*)—to speak of Persons of Opposite Sex Sharing Living Quarters. So the famously bow-tied *CBS Sunday Morning* commentator Charles Osgood penned this tongue-in-cheek poem. The curious new term described a large and growing segment of conjugal couplehood.

Osgood zeroed in on the primary unique factor of cohabiting relationships—their conditional nature: "You'll share my life, *up to a point*! And that you'll be so glad to do." This is what cohabitation is—a domestic and sexual living arrangement quite different from what a man and woman do when they marry.

But is there any significant difference between the two, besides that one is a legal commitment and the other merely a personal agreement? Does it really matter how couples establish and arrange their relationships? Doesn't it just come down to personal preference and what seems to suit the couple? Isn't it really the couple's love that makes the relationship?

These are questions all couples should consider—whether they think they might ever cohabit or not. Finding good answers to them helps us understand the nature of domestic and sexual relationships—something most of us find ourselves entering into.

The Ring Makes All the Difference is a careful, practical look at what we know about couples who choose to live together outside of marriage—and how this knowledge can help create current and future relationships that are as healthy, fulfilling, and long-lasting as possible. *Isn't that what most of us are after?*

The good news is that the psychological and social sciences know a great deal about cohabiting relationships, given that we have seen large and socially diverse populations entering such relationships since the late 1960s. For this is what the social sciences need to conduct their research and reach reliable conclusions: (1) large, diverse populations to observe and (2) many decades to observe them.

It would be difficult to overstate how dramatically cohabiting relationships have grown in most Western nations, including the United States. When it comes to the ways men and women today start and organize their domestic lives, cohabitation is the faraway winner in terms of sheer numerical growth. In family formation trends over the past four decades, the increase of unmarried cohabitation has no close rival:

- Since 1960, the number of cohabiting couples in the US has increased fifteen-fold.[2]
- This growth has been particularly dramatic over the past two decades, with the percentage of cohabiting couples increasing about 50 percent since the mid-1990s and more than doubling in real numbers over these years.[3]
- Today, more than 60 percent of all marriages are preceded by some form of cohabitation. Second marriages are even more likely to be preceded by either partner having lived with someone without a wedding first.[4]

But not all young couples are cohabiting at the same rates. There are important class distinctions. The National Marriage Project reported in 2010 that among women in the twenty-five to forty-four age range, 75 percent of those who never completed high school have cohabited, compared to 50 percent of college graduates. Cohabitation is also more common among those who are less religious than their peers, those who have been divorced, and those who have experienced parental divorce, fatherlessness, or high levels of marital discord during childhood.[5]

POSSLQs are spreading like wildfire. On the next page you will find a chart that plots the remarkable growth trend of cohabitation in the United States since 1960.

BABIES BEFORE WEDDING BELLS

Having interviewed many young adult women over the past decade, I have talked with more than a few who had babies out of wedlock. These are not just young teens or early twentysomething women who got

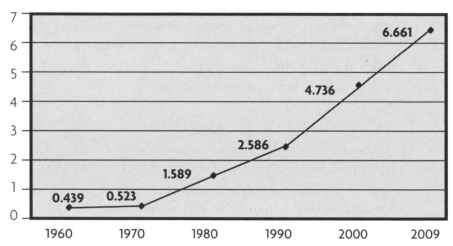

Number (in millions) of US Cohabitating Couples by Year

pregnant by accident. Many are women in their later twenties, thirties, and even early forties who got pregnant intentionally because they found their biological clocks ticking faster than their wedding bells were ringing.

As one successful professional woman living in Seattle, Washington—working as a professor of literature at a noted university—explained to me, she always wanted to get married and have children in the traditional way, but a husband never materialized. She didn't want to miss out on her dream of having children, so she built her motherhood on the prospects of in vitro fertilization. She was not happy it turned out this way, but she is overjoyed with her two-year-old daughter. It is a world she never expected. And she is not alone. The data shows she is a part of a quickly growing demographic.

Unmarried childbearing is cohabitation's closest competitor in terms of growth in the United States. But this has been greatly increased by cohabitation itself, as of all women who give birth outside marriage:

- 56 percent aged 20 to 24,
- 52 percent aged 25 to 28,
- 59 percent aged 30 to 34

have births in nonmarital cohabiting relations.[6] And births to single mothers are greatest among women in their mid- to later twenties, thirties, and even early forties—rather than among teens and young twenties.

This dramatic growth of unmarried childbearing among adult women is largely due to women choosing to have babies with men who are good enough as live-in partners—good enough, they sense, to be baby-daddies, but not good enough to be marriage material. You probably have friends who are there—or have been there.

HOW DID COHABITATION START?

While cohabitation didn't start out this way, living together has seen explosive growth as boys fail or refuse to become men—while still getting what they want from their female peers who desire husbands: companionship, regular sex, and someone to cook and clean for them. We will look in chapter 7 at how women fare in the cohabitation deal compared to their boyfriends.

The cohabitation trend started decades ago, primarily in the Scandinavian countries, spreading across central and northwestern Europe, then to Canada and the United States. Australia and New Zealand have also seen sharp increases over the past twenty years. Of course, this means that marriage rates in these nations have been dropping.

This is because, "There has been little increase in recent times in the propensity of young people to desire to 'become couples,'" says groundbreaking family sociologist David Popenoe.[7] The desire to be a part of a couple has always been high, for a basic human desire is to share our lives and ourselves with an opposite sex partner. But in past decades more couples have been making the choice for cohabitation rather than marriage. The chart on the next page records the recent decline of marriage in the United States.

COHABITATION HAS A LONG HISTORY

While we have seen an explosion of cohabitation in the United States, the concept is not new. It has always been a small part of our culture, since

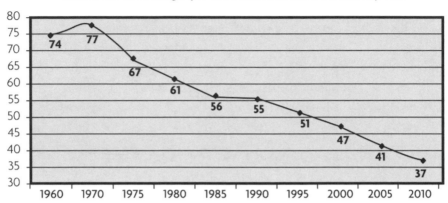

Number of US Marriages per 1,000 Unmarried Adult Women by Year

colonial days. This was primarily true because of the nature of the colonies themselves, rather than people's attitudes.

Many couples lived together—forming home and family outside of legal marriage—not because they didn't believe marriage was important or desirable, but because ministers and magistrates were in short supply in some colonial and postrevolutionary outposts. Others—even if they were not formally married—considered themselves very much married and were viewed that way by their families and neighbors. This is where the concept of "common-law" marriages arose—when a couple considered themselves wedded and showed themselves this way to the larger community, even if they did not have an official ceremony or marriage certificate. These were also called "informal marriages." All that many jurisdictions required for such marriages was a testimony to the exchange of vows—from the couple and possibly family or friends—and then sexual consummation of the union.

In the decades before and after the American Revolution, "significant numbers of marriages were private or departed in significant ways from church sanctioned marriage patterns," says sociological historian Arland Thornton.[8] One clergyman, John Miller, traveling through the New York colonies in the late 1600s complained that so "many couples live together without ever being married in any manner of way."[9] But still these numbers remained relatively low. Recent research shows that for people born before 1928 and reaching early adulthood before World War II, the cohabiting rate was just 2 percent.[10] The kind of cohabitation we saw arise in Western cultures in the 1960s has a very different nature. Rather than lack of officials to perform official commitments, the large and growing numbers of couples living together today has been motivated by two different views of marriage: one high and one low.

THE LOW VIEW OF MARRIAGE

This view was responsible for launching cohabitation as a growing domestic arrangement out of the 1960s sexual revolution. It was motivated by the opinion that legal marriage was an unnecessary—or even stifling—formality that would only spoil the passionate, "pure" love of a young couple.

These cohabitors saw themselves as revolutionaries, explaining their actions with the decree that "love will keep us together" as the popular song proclaimed. Other cohabitors boasted, "We don't need a piece of paper from city hall to make our love meaningful." If they stayed together just because some legal form said they must, what kind of love would that be?

Some people really believed this. Others saw it as a high-minded justification for not having to commit, to keep their options open, to not have to grow up so quickly. This perspective took a low view of marriage because it reduced marriage to just the legal contract, merely a "piece of paper." In this view, what really mattered was the couple's love.

With its romantic, idealistic appeal, this view caught on with young people throughout the '70s and '80s. But during this time, young people still reported to scholars that marriage and family were their most important life goals—and that gaining a spouse and having children were very important in living a happy, fulfilling life.

They believed this, even while they were cohabiting in growing numbers. It is not the first time that young adults would exhibit an inconsistency between what they said they believed and what they actually did. It is, perhaps, one of the perks of being young.

THE HIGH VIEW OF MARRIAGE

Another, more recent view surprisingly takes a high view of marriage. *How could a high view of marriage prompt couples to cohabit?* Let me explain.

The cohabitors of the '90s and the first decade of the twenty-first century do not have the earlier "who needs a piece of paper?" attitude. They are not motivated by the idea that cohabitation is a purer, nobler relationship than marriage. Instead, they have a crippling fear of failure in what they are so desperately looking for. And what they are looking for is largely what they were denied by their parents' lives.

Fear

Gen Xers, and those coming after them, saw their parents divorce in record numbers. And guess what? Unlike what so many of their parents were told, they didn't see this as a powerful, healthy, liberating event.[11] Most speak of their parents' divorce as a deeply painful and defining event in their lives. Devastating. Many call it dramatically "scarring" and the end of their childhood.

The individual and collective pain of their generation would be difficult to exaggerate. Generations tend to be shaped by what they were denied. The generation raised during the Depression became remarkably prosperous. The generation raised in the family solidity of the '40s and '50s ushered in the experimentation and family upheaval of the '60s and '70s. These are not coincidences.

Young people today deeply desire marriage because of the family breakdown brought by their parents' experimentation. A new sophisticated report from the Pew Research Center on the state of marriage in America reports Millennials have "the strongest desire to marry" of any generation alive today.[12] This is not just happenstance. And they desperately don't want to muck up the carpet of marriage with their relational anxiety, dysfunction, or the bad relational mojo they inherited from their parents. They very much want to get it right. They feel they *must* get it right. Therefore, cohabiting, they figure, may be the best they can do—and it provides an easy exit if either partner sabotages the relationship.

As one young African-American woman who works as a theater set designer in the Atlanta area told me, "When we see the statistics, we are scared witless at the possibility of failing at what we want so badly: marriage. So it makes it hard for us to make the plunge."

As a Placeholder

She was a nice girl from a good Christian home. She knew right from wrong, but she also knew she wanted to start her own life free from her parents' model. She hadn't yet found "Mr. Right." But she had met a nice young man at school whom she thought could be a good partner to help her navigate the pressure-ridden, sometimes lonely college years. They moved in together and lived as a couple through her freshman and sophomore years. Her parents were not happy with the arrangement, but she didn't let that bother her. She was an adult and could make her own decisions. At least that's how she worked it out in her mind.

Not all young couples today are motivated by a fear of failure. Others desire a domestic partnership, but haven't found that special one to whom they want to make a life commitment. So for the time being, they cohabit as a relational placeholder. And they figure it might serve as a good training ground for marriage.

Scholars at the Institute for Social Research at the University of Michigan report that fewer than one-fourth of first-time cohabitors today have no interest in ever marrying, nor see cohabitation as a possible testing ground for future marriage. The other three-fourths have some plans for marriage and see their current relationship as a step toward that. As recently as the late 1980s, only half of cohabitors said their relationship was some sort of preparation for marriage.[13] This is a dramatic shift. Who would have thought that today's cohabitors are highly marriage minded?

Most cohabitors today have the intention, if not the strong desire, to marry someday. They see their relationship as one that may help move them in that direction. And young adults are very likely (62 percent) to believe that "living together with someone before marriage is a good way to avoid an eventual divorce."[14]

CAN COHABITATION FULFILL ITS PROMISE?

So here is one of the most important questions we seek to answer in this book:

How likely is it that living together before marriage will help you reach your goal of a happy, thriving, and fulfilling relationship leading to marriage?

How fulfilling is cohabitation? This is an important question, given how valuable young people say marriage is to them. According to what they say, they would like one day to be happily married, having found a good mate to share their life with, raise a gaggle of beautiful children together, and grow old with each other, hand in hand, life entwined with life.

PEOPLE today don't
have to wonder how
living together might work out,
for we can learn from the experiences
of those who have already tried it.

Couples who are considering moving in together should ask themselves this question because there are strong and reliable answers they can gain from the experience of millions of cohabitors who have already gone down that road.

People today don't have to wonder how living together might work out, for we can learn from the experiences of those who have already tried it.

In these pages you won't hear the voices of parents or pastors giving their advice about what *they* think is right. You will learn from what the world's leading social scientists have discovered through careful research, studying and observing those who have cohabited before marriage in various situations over the past four decades. They have tested their findings and submitted them to the review of their professional peers. Their findings have been published in scholarly journals and are now carefully catalogued here for your benefit.

You don't need a graduate degree in sociology to understand what they have found. I have taken care to explain it for you in plain language.

This book is written for you to smooth the way in finding the smart answers you need. It is my desire that you have the insight you need to make wise decisions so you can create the healthiest, happiest, most fulfilling relationships available—so you can be wise in following both your *heart* and your *head* in this important life decision.

QUESTIONS
for Couples

I. What are you looking for in life regarding your own family relationships?

2. Do you have a high or a low view of marriage? What about your partner?

3. If you are considering cohabitation, honestly list your personal reasons for choosing this option. What are the relational benefits you believe it will achieve for you?

4. What are your fears or concerns about entering a cohabiting relationship?

5. People are products of their heritage. What is the marriage story of your family of origin? What kind of marital history, success or failure, did your parents have? What about your partner? What was the marital history of your grandparents? What about your partner's grandparents?

6. How do you think the generational history of marriage in your family has affected your attitudes toward marriage? How has it done so in positive ways and in negative ways?

7. How do you think your partner's attitudes toward marriage have been affected by his or her family's marital history? (Have your partner answer the same question for you—and discuss this between you. This can be very helpful.)

RECOMMENDED RESOURCES

David Popenoe and Barbara Dafoe Whitehead, "Should We Live Together?" A report of the National Marriage Project, University of Virginia, 2002. The twenty-four-page report can be found at: http://www.virginia.edu/marriageproject/pdfs/swlt2.pdf

NOTES

1. Charles Osgood, *There's Nothing That I Wouldn't Do if You Would Be My POSSLQ* (New York: Holt, Rinehart & Winston, 1981).

2. W. Bradford Wilcox and Elizabeth Marquardt, "When Marriage Disappears: The New Middle America," The State of Our Unions, 2010, an annual report on marriage in America from the National Marriage Project (Charlotte, VA: University of Virginia, December 2010), 76.

3. David Popenoe, *Cohabitation, Marriage and Wellbeing: A Cross National Perspective* (Rutgers University, the National Marriage Project, 2008), 2.

4. Sheila Kennedy and Larry Bumpass, "Cohabitation and Children's Living Arrangements: New Estimates from the United States," *Demographic Research* 19 (2008): 1663–92; Paul R. Amato, Alan Booth, David R. Johnson, Stacy J. Rogers, *Alone Together: How Marriage in America is Changing* (Cambridge, MA: Harvard University Press, 2007), 21; Arland Thornton, William G. Axinn, and Yu Xie, *Marriage and Cohabitaion* (Chicago: University of Chicago Press, 2007), 72.

5. Wilcox and Marquardt, 2010, 76.

6. W. Bradford Wilcox, "The Evolution of Divorce," *National Affairs*, autumn 2009, 7; Lisa Mincieli et al., "The Relationship Context of Births Outside of Marriage: The Rise of Cohabitation," *Child Trends Research Brief*, May 2007, figure 4, 3.

7. Popenoe, 2008, 3.

8. Thornton et al., 2007, 42.

9. Richard Godbeer, *Sexual Revolution in Early America* (Baltimore: Johns Hopkins University Press, 2002), 8.

10. Larry L. Bumpass and James A. Sweet, "National Estimates of Cohabitation," *Demography* 26 (1989): 615–25.

11. Barbara Dafoe Whitehead, *The Divorce Culture* (New York: Alfred A. Knopf, 1997).

12. Pew Research Center, "The Decline of Marriage and the Rise of New Families," Pew Charitable Trust, November 2010, 36.

13. Thornton et al., 2007, 87.

14. Andrew J. Cherlin, *The Marriage-Go-Round: The State of Marriage and the Family in America Today* (New York: Alfred A. Knopf, 2009), 139.

MARRIAGE matters,

not just because it is preceded by a

wedding that costs us or our parents

tens of thousands of dollars, but

because the nature of the relationship

itself makes a difference in ways you

probably never imagined.

2

WHAT ARE WE LOOKING FOR IN RELATIONSHIPS?

> We don't want freedom,
> we don't want justice,
> we just want someone to love!
> —Louis Fine,
> in the movie *True Stories*

ONE OF THE MOST PROFOUND statements in all of human literature is found in the second chapter of an ancient, tried-and-true book. It is an observation made about human beings.

The book is the biblical book of Genesis. The observation is God's.

As He looks upon His perfect and amazing creation—the splendor of the Swiss Alps, the azure Caribbean and the South Pacific, the warm African savannas, and all the amazing creatures and plants that inhabit the land and savannas—God recognizes that something was not good.

How could something in God's grand creation not be good? Nothing had yet happened to spoil it. But this is what God says. Something was not as it should be. In Genesis 2:18 God says:

"It is not good for the man to be alone . . ."

Think about this profound statement. Repeat it slowly to yourself.

This is perhaps the most defining, basic statement about humanity. But did God make a mistake? Is that why something in the perfection of creation is not good?

No, nothing got past God. He didn't make a mistake.

He is explaining something deeply fundamental about the first human being He created—and therefore something important about all human beings. This is true of you, me, and everyone else we will ever know. In fact, it is the *second* most fundamental truth about us. And it stems from the first.

God is teaching us that humanity is created to be the only part of creation made in the image and likeness of God. Genesis 1:26 says:

"Let us make man in our image, in our likeness . . ."

This is the second truth. What is the *first*? It is this: God, while being one God, is not solitary. He is Trinity and is therefore one God as a community of three divine persons: Father, Son, and Holy Spirit.

What practical difference does this make? Actually, all the difference in the universe, quite literally. Hang with me on this. It explains what each of us—and the universe—is all about. See if this is not true about you.

Jesus explains the essence of the divine Godhead to us in His prayer to the Father the evening before He goes to the cross. In John 17:24, Jesus says:

"Father . . . you loved me before the creation of the world."

Before anything existed, before anything was created. . . there was love, between a Father and a Son.

The Holy Trinity is marked by love—their fundamental character quality, their primary nature. First John 4:8 tells us, "God is Love." So to be created in the image of the God who is Trinitarian love means to be created for love, relationship, and intimacy. Therefore we all desire it, we all seek it. In fact, we all require it. There is no escaping this fact. And you are no different.

This is why it was not good for man to be alone. He was not created to be alone. In his aloneness, he does not represent the nature of God.

But this fundamental human problem was solved in the first human community—the relationship between a man and a woman. By himself—without someone similar to him, sharing his humanity but also different from him—man cannot love like God does. This is big.

God the Father is the *Other* of God the Son. God the Son is the *Other* of the Father. And they both are the *Other* of the Holy Spirit and likewise. Each is God—divine, but distinctly different in meaningful ways.

Adam, in his solitude, did not have an *other*, as God has always had in His Trinity. For a male, female is that *other*, and vice versa. This may sound a little philosophical, but it matters in big ways for our most basic desire.

To be loving, we must have a beloved. Love demands an object. And for Adam to be a God-imager, this *other* would have to be like him, sharing his humanity, but also distinctly different from him.

At first Adam did not have this, and therefore it was not good. What solved this fundamental human problem? "She shall be called 'woman'" (Genesis 2:23). Woman is God's answer to man's—to humanity's—most fundamental problem. *This makes woman not only pretty important, but absolutely amazing.*

This is not just a quaint Bible story, like our Sunday school teachers taught us with flannel boards and coloring books. This is one of the heaviest truths humans can contemplate. It illustrates the first fundamental truth about God—and therefore about each of us. We are *for* others. We must be. And we will not find contentment and wholeness without relationship.

THE UNBEARABLE PAIN OF LONELINESS

No human can withstand loneliness. There is a reason it devastates us. To say we need others is not just to speak of a preference. It is a deep, gnawing human need. As Louis Fine, the affable but searching character played by John Goodman in one of my favorite quirky movies, *True Stories*, says, "We all want someone to love."

We all *need* someone to love. Popular music, movies, and literature are full of this message for bigger reasons than the mere fact that it sells.

It is what Morrissey of the alternative band The Smiths sang about in their haunting 1984 hit "How Soon Is Now?" In the beautiful song he explained that he is human and he needs to be loved, just like everyone else does.

Morrissey may not have understood the significance of the Christian theology of the Trinity, but he realized its consequences.

It's what indie pop singer Ingrid Michaelson sang to us in her 2009 song "Everybody." What does everybody want? Simple in her mind. Everybody wants to be loved. There are no exceptions. And if we think we have found one, we will find the person delusional, deeply disturbed, mentally ill. You can bank on it!

It is what the director of the wonderful film *Castaway* wanted us to understand when Tom Hanks's character Chuck Nolan, while stranded alone for years on a remote island, came to be profoundly attached to a new friend, a volleyball named Wilson.

It is what Jon Krakauer illustrated in his book *Into the Wild* (made into a movie by the same name, directed by Sean Penn). The privileged Christopher McCandless, after graduating from Emory University, gave away all of his possessions, said good-bye to family and friends, and went to live as a recluse in the Alaskan wilderness. But after less than a year he realized— while reading *Dr. Zhivago*—that no human can survive such isolation, even if he could provide himself with ample food and shelter. True happiness, he came to learn, is experienced only in relationship with others.

I don't think McCandless knew the truth of God as Trinity and that we are created in His image. But he learned it from a great work of literature. And literature, as well as other works of art, often point us to the truth of God because they speak of His creation.

We cannot be alone. Needing others is our most fundamental human need. That is how God made us.

WHAT WE NEED AND WANT

So, given this fundamental human need—found both in human psychology and sacred Scripture—what are we looking for today in our relationships? What we are all looking for . . . are those qualities we have always been looking for:

- We want relationship, someone to spend our time with.
- We want companionship.
- We want real love.
- We want to be understood.
- We want to be valued—to be significant to another.
- We want someone to share our life—our happiness and our tears.
- We want someone to be there when we come home at night.
- We want someone to rely on, to do life's daily chores with.
- We want sexual intimacy.
- We want someone to confide in—and for them to confide in us.
- We want someone we can try to make happy and be there for.
- We want someone who needs us.
- We want someone who knows us like no other.
- We want someone who is comfortable—who makes us laugh.
- We want someone who wants to help us be better.
- We want someone who can give it to us straight—but with love.
- We want someone we can dump on from time to time.
- We want someone we can trust and give ourselves to completely: emotionally, physically, sexually, materially.
- We want someone who will not let us settle for what's easy.
- We want someone we feel would give up anything for us.
- We want someone who will never give up on us.
- We want someone *we* will never give up on.
- We want someone who is crazy about us.
- We want someone who will be there.
- We want someone to become a parent with.
- We want someone who is not just in it for themself.

Doesn't this describe you? Doesn't it describe everyone around you? Is there anyone you know who doesn't want these things, who is perfectly satisfied without them?

If so, is that a person you really want to know?

Has anyone truly disagreed with that famous line from *It's a Wonderful Life*: "No man is a failure who has friends"? We know of plenty of people who had power, influence, prestige—nice things—but died sad and lonely because they didn't know how to truly love others.

We are made for others. While we experience our greatest wounds at the hands of others, they are also the source of our greatest joys and contentment. In an episode in the second season of *30 Rock*, Jack Donaghy (played by Alec Baldwin) experiences a serious heart ailment that lands him in the hospital, seemingly at the edge of death. But the real source of his discomfort was the news of his overbearing mother's visit. With what he thinks is his last breath, he says he is anguished by so many crippling regrets. He tells Tina Fey's character Liz Lemon that chief among them is that he didn't spend enough time at work. The humor lies in the silliness that we know *no one* says that on their deathbed. They regret not investing more of themselves with the ones they love.

People need people—and couples are looking to satisfy that need in the most intimate and long-term ways. It is very natural.

DO MEN AND WOMEN
HAVE DIFFERENT GOALS?

In my work, I get to speak to lots of young couples about the nature of their relationships. I hear about their successes and failures, their strengths and weaknesses, their wishes and dreams. I often hear the same sort of things, but communicated in a zillion different ways. Sometimes what men say and what woman say are similar. But often they are different. Men are looking for specific things, while women are looking for different specific things.

Sometimes men just want to be left alone. Sometimes women just want to be listened to. Men are more interested in fulfilling their most basic appetites:

- somewhat regular sex
- warm food and cold beverages

- interesting entertainment
- fulfilling work.

More times than not, that is the male satisfaction quad. Get these things right, and the man is generally content.

Women, in general, are more interested in fulfilling their relational desires:

- closeness
- connecting
- sharing
- intimacy
- a sense of meaningfulness.

Get these things right for the woman, and she is usually good to go.

Men are interested in adventure of many different sorts. Women desire security. Men are hunter-gatherers. Women more often are shoppers-browsers. Both find comfort in routine. But both occasionally like to deviate from the everyday.

Both like surprises and special things done for them, but in different ways. Both want to know they don't have to carry the whole load all the time. Both want grace and forgiveness. Men need to be needed. Women want to be considered, to be thought of.[1]

What are we looking for in our relationships? Consider the stories of these four couples.

SHE WANTS SECURITY; HE WANTS RESPECT

Tina and Manuel, a married couple living just north of San Diego, are working their way through college and have nearly full-time jobs. They want to be able to enjoy time together when they don't have to worry about their schoolwork or keeping up with their small house.

Tina wants to know Manuel is applying himself to his studies because she wants to be a mom someday and not have to work full-time, particularly when the kids are young. She was a latchkey kid growing up, and she wants something different for their little ones. So Tina needs a sense of security from Manuel and his career. Most of her girlfriends, she says, have a similar desire.

Manuel needs to know Tina believes in him—that she has faith he can complete his studies and find a good job in veterinary medicine. This is the source of his greatest sense of self-confidence. "I could turn the world on its head if Tina believes I can," Manuel says, "but I couldn't lift that stack of schoolbooks if she's not behind me. It is amazing how much her belief in me matters."

For each to be able to achieve their personal goal, they also need their partner to reach theirs. This is what makes their relationship so important to them.

SHE WANTS TRUST,
HE WANTS TO FIX

During Margo's childhood in Chile, her father was spectacularly unfaithful to her mother. Margo loved her daddy, but she also thought—knew—he was a pig. He didn't even try to hide his selfish sins. And her mom never seemed to raise an objection, which left Margo with contempt for both her parents. Was her mom insecure, ignorant, or unfeeling? Margo didn't know.

When Margo met her first really serious boyfriend, she had to know he would remain faithful, that he would be a man she and their future children could depend on. But even years after they married, she still has trouble believing Tommy can keep his promise of fidelity. She also knows her worries arise much more because of her background than because of Tommy.

While Tommy understands Margo's fears, his commitment and amazing consideration have not satisfied his wife's anxiety. She is gradually learning to trust that men can be faithful, but it has not been easy. Tommy remains angry toward his father-in-law for what he instilled in Margo and how this affects Tommy's relationship with her.

But Tommy is committed to being a different kind of father to his children. And Margo desperately needs to see—to experience—this. It is what she yearns for. Tommy feels a sense of mission in giving Margo a different experience, as well as breaking that legacy for his children.

HE WANTS WARMTH; SHE WANTS TO BE MORE THAN A SECURITY BLANKET

Reggie grew up in a caring family in Singapore, but one that rarely showed physical affection. He could not remember being cuddled when he was small or sitting on either parent's laps for closeness, warmth, and security.

So when Reggie met Martif, he had to work to not respond as a bone-dry intimacy sponge. He always had to be touching her in some way—holding her hand, placing his hand on her knee, having his arm touching hers as they sat in church. He needed some flesh-to-flesh connection, no matter how minimal. For Reggie, this provided a deeply needed sense of security.

But while Martif loved Reggie deeply, his neediness made her feel objectified—not in a sexual way but more like a child's teddy bear or security blanket. Martif wanted to be his lover, his wife, the mother of his children. She desired to be a woman to him, not his mommy. Reggie had to work on treating his wife like a woman, his partner, his lover. They both wanted this, but it was a struggle.

SHE WANTS DEPENDABILITY; HE WANTS FREEDOM

Leon and Michelle hope to get married when she graduates with her master's degree in social psychology. She wants to go into law enforcement management. Leon frames houses for a local contractor in Toronto and stays plenty busy.

They moved in together last semester, a year after they met, to save on expenses. Leon was at her place nearly all the time, so it seemed to make sense. Why pay rent on another apartment just so they wouldn't have to admit to his parents that they were living together? And Michelle says it helps her to have someone to come home to and at least be there while she studies and prepares for the classes she teaches as her professor's assistant.

But she doesn't like that Leon's friend Rich comes over so much because he eats all their snacks and is an addicted gamer. These guys spend hours on both activities. It's not the kind of study atmosphere Michelle needs, and she doesn't care for Rich's influence on Leon. His friend isn't helping Leon become the man she wants him to be.

Something has to give. But Leon sees Michelle's request for Rich-free evenings as being controlling. After all, Rich is his best bud. He knew him long before he knew her.! They're both left wondering what kinds of compromises are called for in their relationship.

A SPECIAL KIND OF RELATIONSHIP

We all look for relationship, but we're also looking for a certain type of relationship—a long-term, for-life, most-intimate relationship where we go to bed and wake up with that one special person. A relationship where we share our home with them, enjoy our meals, do our chores, keep a budget, and share our lives. A relationship where we build a lasting life together.

So are there any important differences between certain types of domestic and sexual relationships and how they provide what we are looking for in our pursuit of contentment? Do different kinds of relationships make a difference in our ability to give ourselves totally to the one we love?

ARE some types

of relationships more or less

likely to contribute to

a happy, fulfilling life for us,

our partner, and our children?

These are the primary questions we will consider in this book. Are some types of relationships—particularly marriage and living together before or instead of marriage—more or less likely to contribute to a happy, fulfilling life for us, our partner, and our children than other types of relationships?

Does it really matter?

According to the life wishes of young adults today, it does.

When the Pew Research Center conducted a major study of the attitudes of Americans toward marriage and other forms of relationships, they discovered there is a strong feeling—especially among young people—as to what kind of relationships are most likely to lead to fulfilling, happy lives.

Based on their findings, cohabitors themselves are more likely to say they want to marry—even more than those who are single. I find it curious that cohabitors are more likely than others to yearn for marriage. And 69 percent of current cohabitors believe they will one day marry, while only 25 percent say they have no interest in marrying.[2] If cohabitation is a satisfying replacement for marriage, these numbers show the young adults forming relationships today haven't gotten the message.

SLIDING VS. DECIDING?

So why do we continue to see cohabitation rapidly growing, while marriage steadily declines? Primarily because we realize marriage is a higher-order relationship. Living together outside of marriage requires less commitment and effort. It is easier to leave if we feel it's not working. Marriage is different. It is a more serious commitment, requiring more of us, for ourselves and our spouse. And marriage, unlike cohabitation, involves our extended families.

Also, while more couples are choosing to cohabit, they are not *deciding* to cohabit. Sound odd? Let me explain.

Scott Stanley of the University of Denver, one of a handful of scholars breaking important research ground on the topic of cohabitation, has coined a phrase to describe how many cohabiting relationships are formed: "sliding vs. deciding."[3] He draws on a 2005 finding that just over

50 percent of cohabiting couples do not report any kind of deliberate decision process in their choosing to move in together.[4]

For most of these couples, cohabiting just sort of happens, rather than coming from a deliberate decision such as, "Why don't we get our lives organized, find a nice place downtown, and move in together next fall." Cohabitors are more likely, these scholars are finding, to just *slide* into their live-in relationships.

This distinction is important, Stanley explains, because *deciding* is a protective factor in making important life choices, but *sliding* is not.[5] People are more likely to put effort into something they decide to do, rather than what they just fall into.

And, as we'll examine in chapter 7, cohabitors who do eventually marry are more likely to just "slide" into marriage because of the relational inertia created by cohabiting. This is because cohabitors, even in less-than-fulfilling relationships, find it more difficult to break off the relationship and not marry than if they were simply dating and discussing marriage. This is just one of the reasons why marriages formed after cohabitation are found to be less healthy than other marriages.

EFFORT VS. OUTCOME

We are more likely to desire something that requires more of us, even while we might fear making that commitment and putting in the hard work. We know that greater devotion and self-sacrifice are more likely to produce the kind of happiness in life that we seek. But it is hard to take that dive when we are increasingly unsure about our ability to make it work.

Perhaps one thing that can help us make the greater commitment that marriage requires is to realize how much better marriage does at bringing an array of important things to our lives—things that cohabitation cannot and does not produce.

Marriage matters—not just because it is preceded by a glorious wedding that costs us or our parents tens of thousands of dollars—but because the nature of the relationship itself makes a difference in ways you never imagined. Respected sociologists and psychologists from various ideological backgrounds are discovering the nature of our domestic and sexual relationships matters far beyond the sentimental. It is not personal choice that matters most. We can definitively and confidently say that some forms of relationship are measurably better than others. Significantly better. We will explore in the next four chapters what science is revealing to us about the natures and qualities of marital and cohabiting relationships.

QUESTIONS
for Couples

1. Discuss with your partner what you are both looking for in your relationship. List, in descending priority, your five most important things. Be honest about your expectations.

2. How different are your expectations? How similar?

3. Do you think men and women really have different expectations for their domestic and sexual relationships? Why or why not?

4. What is it about being a man or a woman that might drive these different expectations?

5. In the beginning of this chapter, we looked at how our need for relationship is rooted in our being created in the image of God. How does this view affect your view of either marriage or cohabitation? What practical difference do you think it might make?

6. What are some ways you could see how *sliding* into cohabitation, rather than *deciding* for marriage, could influence the quality and nature of your relationship?

RECOMMENDED RESOURCES

Sliding vs Deciding.com—a blog of University of Denver professor Professor Scott Stanley looking at the importance of commitment in marriage and romantic relationships.
http://slidingvsdeciding.blogspot.com/

NOTES

1. Glenn T. Stanton, *Secure Daughters, Confident Sons: How Parents Guide Their Children into Authentic Masculinity and Feminity* (Colorado Springs: Multnomah, 2011), chapters 3 and 4.

2. Pew Research Center, "The Decline of Marriage and the Rise of New Families," Pew Charitable Trust, November 2010, 92.

3. Scott M. Stanley, Galena Kline Rhoades, and Howard J. Markman, "Sliding vs. Deciding: Inertia and the Premarital Cohabitation Effect," *Family Relations* 55 (2006): 499–509.

4. Wendy D. Manning and Pamela J. Smock, "Measuring and Modeling Cohabitation: New Perspectives from Qualitative Data," *Journal of Marriage and Family* 67 (2005): 989–1002.

5. Scott Stanley and Galena K. Rhoades, "Sliding vs. Deciding: Understanding a Mystery," *Family Focus*, a newsletter of the National Council on Family Relations (Issue FF42), summer 2009, f3.

EVEN if couples consider

themselves essentially "married," they

know that without a marriage license,

they are freer to exit the relationship at

any time. This lack of security in the

mind of each partner affects

how they deal with each other.

3

HOW COHABITING RELATIONSHIPS DIFFER FROM MARRIAGE

TODD AND LESLIE LIVE on the northeast side of Dallas in a lovely town house near a new golf community. While they live in an upscale area, they are not wealthy. With their jobs as a nurse and a junior member of a law firm, they do well to keep up with their bills and repay school loans. Todd is the nurse, and Leslie is the lawyer. Their friends kid them about their lack of gender stereotyping. But Todd, who can bench more than three hundred pounds, never lets the ribbing go too far. But by most standards, they have a nice life.

Steve and Terry also live in the Dallas area. Terry is a manager with American Airlines, and Steve is a successful car salesman at a large Honda dealership. They both live close to work, avoiding long commutes on the twisted spaghetti of Dallas freeways. Both sets of parents live close by.

Both couples are similar in terms of their social standing, their prospects for the future, and their desires for their families. Both want children, but not quite yet.

Both couples are in the early stages of their lives together. Steve and Terry have been married for nine months. Todd and Leslie moved in together ten months ago. Both couples dated for six or seven months before making their big moves.

Both couples are well educated and have secure, respectable jobs. But are their relationships really similar? Other than Steve and Terry being an interracial (Hispanic/Asian) couple and their different marital statuses, it seems they are pretty much mirror image couples. Does the fact that one has a marriage license and the other does not make any practical difference in their lives? Does it just come down to tomato/tomahto or potato/potahto—two different ways of looking at essentially the same thing? They both seem crazy in love with one another and enjoy each other's company, sharing their lives together.

WE CAN KNOW THE ANSWERS

Those of us asking these questions today are fortunate to have a robust body of social, psychological, and even medical science to learn from. In the 1970s, we didn't have this insight. So it was just assumed that if the couple was truly in love, and they had decent jobs and a real commitment to one another, what else could possibly be needed? The marriage license seemed a mere formality. But we no longer have to depend on assumptions. Social scientists need two things to be able to draw strong, reliable conclusions:

1. They need large, diverse populations to study so they can test for and consider lots of factors such as ethnic and racial differences as well as geographic and socioeconomic variables.
2. They need long periods of time—decades if possible—to collect long-term measures then examine, analyze, and test the data against the findings of other scholars.

With the explosive growth of cohabitation over the past four decades among couples in many cultures and life situations, scientists have an abundance of both. So they have been able to reach some very interesting and reliable conclusions.

Therefore, couples today considering marriage or cohabitation can make informed decisions about what type of relationship is more likely to lead to the happiness, intimacy, and longevity they seek. Smart couples will make use of such an opportunity.

In this and the next three chapters, we will consult this impressive body of research to learn how different marriage and cohabiting relationships actually are in very practical and important ways. In this chapter, we start with some of the primary differences between relationships built on the foundation of cohabitation and those built on marriage.

THE VERY PRACTICAL DIFFERENCES

The first big difference is the most obvious. The glue holding the relationship together is different. Even if couples consider themselves essentially "married" while still cohabiting, they know that without a marriage license and wedding rings, they are freer to exit the relationship at any time. And this lack of security is there in the minds of each partner. It affects how they deal with each other. Consider this scenario:

Her: *Jim, be sure to keep Saturday open. It's my niece's birthday, and Robin and Hawk are having her birthday party at Chunks-O-Cheese Pizza. They were wondering if you could dress up in a Barney costume they are renting and appear for the kids. I told them you would probably be happy to help.*

Him: *Now Susan, as much as I like your niece, there are two problems. First, if I wanted to spend my Saturdays sweating in a purple dinosaur suit, I'd be working for an amusement park. Second, I already made plans to go fishing with Rick. His dad is letting him use his boat, and the snapper are coming in.*

Her: *Now what do you think is the more important thing to do? Make a little girl happy or go catch some stinky fish? She's practically your niece too.*

Him: *As hard as I work, I do think it is more important for me to go fishing. Brittney will have you there at the party, and she hardly knows me. And she is not my niece. I am not her uncle. Why can't her dad do the Barney thing?*

The negotiating between couples who are married is quite different. As we will see, a wife is a much more powerful player in the relationship than a girlfriend. And marital status matters not just for the couple but also for the extended family. This has many real and practical implications. Jim with a ring on his finger is more likely to do the Barney gig for his niece—and be happier about it—than Jim sans the ring. Scenarios like this come up in domestic relationships in a bundle of different ways. And, as we will see, the ring matters.

Consider the two couples we introduced at the beginning of this chapter. They both want to buy their first home together and stop paying rent. Neither has quite enough for a down payment, but they have both found what they consider the perfect home. But to make the sale, each couple will have to act fast. Both couples decide to do what many others down through the ages have done. They go to their parents to see if they might give them a loan (or a gift!) to help them secure their first home.

Terry suggests they go to her dad to ask for help. He has a modest job, but he has done well in some real estate investments. The newlyweds sit down with him one evening, explain their situation, and ask for his help. Terry knows how to ask her dad for such things. Steve was instructed beforehand to cover just the details of the mortgage and the quality of the home, and after that to keep from saying the wrong thing and leave the rest to her.

Terry's dad paused for a few moments to give the impression he was thinking it over, but he was happy to loan them the $10,000 they needed to make them competitive in the bid for their first home.

Todd and Leslie put together a similar game plan, but they talked to Todd's parents first. Both listened as Todd and Leslie explained their plans. After asking a few searching questions about the deal, Todd's mom spoke up. Todd could tell by the way she looked at his dad that they had already discussed what she would say. And he didn't have a good feeling about it. She explained that while they both were very happy for them in their relationship (and truth be told, Mom was more positive on their relationship than Dad was), they wanted to give the couple more time to see if the relationship was really going to last before they loaned any money. The next night, Leslie's parents said essentially the same thing.

THE COMMITMENT IS
A MESSAGE TO ALL

When the couple themselves have not made a measurable commitment to their relationship, it is unlikely that others will. Todd's and Leslie's parents have no doubt about how their kids feel about their partner—that their love is deeper than it ever has been for anyone. But without the glue of marriage, they don't have enough faith in the strength of their union to invest the money needed for the house. No doubt, either set of parents would do anything for their kids. But in this case, the nature of their relationship makes a real difference. In-law status matters in very practical ways.

MARRIAGE involves things

the cohabiting couple

—or at least one of them—

would rather not deal with.

This is why cohabitation even exists.

The fact that couples choose to cohabit rather than marry indicates there is a difference between the two relationships. Marriage involves things the cohabiting couple—or at least one of them—would rather not deal with. This is why cohabitation even exists.

Marriage requires more up-front and ongoing investment from the spouses and their extended families, notes James Q. Wilson, the veritable dean of social scientists today. Without the process of marriage, "neither the man nor the woman has any strong [or external] incentive to invest heavily in the union," Wilson says. "Marriage is a way of making such investments plausible by telling each party that they are united forever, and if they wish to dissolve this union, they will have to go through an elaborate and possibly costly legal ritual called divorce."[1] This reality is one of the sticking points in the glue of marriage. Another is the friends and family around us.

Marriage "integrates the couple with the larger community" in a way that cohabitation does not, says professor Arland Thornton of the Institute for Social Research at the University of Michigan—one of the world's leading schools of family sociology—in his recent book-length examination of the differences in cohabiting and married couples. Therefore, he finds, "the relationships of cohabitors with parents and others are often quite different from the family relationships of married people."

Thornton explains that numerous studies published from the mid-eighties to the 2000s find that "cohabiting unions are generally not entered into with the same commitment to the permanence of the relationship that characterizes entrance into marriage."[2]

And this is not just the couple's commitment but also the feeling of investment that their friends and family have in the marriage. Others don't have this same feeling of being invested in a cohabiting relationship. Even as cohabiting becomes more common and socially accepted, it has still been shown that cohabiting couples are more likely to be isolated from their circle of friends and family.

And this investment and commitment of marriage affects far more elements in a relationship than getting a home loan or dressing up in a Barney outfit for a little girl's birthday party.

WHICH RELATIONSHIPS ARE HEALTHIER?

All other things being equal, cohabiting relationships are far less healthy than marital relationships in all important measures. This shows up time and again in the best research on the subject. Michael Newcomb and P. M. Bentler, early researchers looking at the psychological nature of cohabiting relationships, discovered that:

Cohabitors experienced significantly more difficulty in their [relationships] with adultery, alcohol, drugs, and independence than couples who had not cohabited. Apparently this makes marriage preceded by cohabitation more prone to problems often associated with other deviant lifestyles—for example, use of drugs and alcohol, more permissive sexual relationships, and an abhorrence of dependence —than marriages not preceded by cohabitation.[3]

Jan Stets, one of the first scholars to make a serious study of cohabiting relationships, found that "cohabiting couples, compared to married couples, have less healthy relationships. They have lower relationship quality, lower stability, and a higher level of disagreements."[4] And while cohabitation has lost much of its social stigma over the past few decades, recent scholars report similar findings,

Cohabitors experience disagreements more often than their married counterparts. Similarly, cohabitors report more fights or violence, as well as lower levels of fairness in their relationships and happiness with them.[5]

These factors are just some of the reasons that cohabitors have breakup rates five times higher than those who are married.[6]

Let's look at some of the specific ways cohabiting relationships prove unhealthy for those who choose to live together before marrying. Let's start with one of the most significant.

SAFETY FROM DOMESTIC VIOLENCE

Given the lack of clarity in cohabiting relationships, it is not surprising that many live-in relationships work out like Mitch and Kendra's. Mitch likes to work on the 1972 GTO he is restoring with his buddy Clint. He works on it a lot—more than Kendra would prefer. And this is one source of friction for the couple.

Mitch says Kendra "acts like his wife," always wanting him to be home and paying attention to her. He says he just wants to live his life.

Kendra thinks that expecting Mitch to stay home a few nights a week is not too much to ask. But this, as Mitch explains it, has led to him "feeling controlled."

And the fevered disagreements over the basic nature of their relationship—who has what kind of claim on the other—has led to violent interactions between the couple. They start with yelling and can quickly lead to shoving and then hitting. Though both tend to initiate the physical contact—which is rare in domestic violence situations—it is Mitch who usually finishes it because of his greater strength.

Careful research over the past few decades into which kinds of relationships experience more violence shows that situations like Mitch and Kendra's are more common among cohabiting couples than among couples who are married. The Family Violence Research Program at the University of New Hampshire, the nation's leading institution studying domestic violence, finds that all other things being equal, "cohabitors are much more violent than marrieds." Specifically, the overall rate of violence for cohabiting couples is twice as high as for married couples, and the rate for "severe" violence is nearly five times greater.[7]

The *Journal of Family Violence* reported on the most common relationship between domestic batterers and victims. "The most frequently cited relationship was cohabitation with close to one half (48 percent) of the couples living together." The lowest rate (19 percent) was found among married couples. Those who were divorced and separated held the middle ranking (27.3 percent).[8]

"Aggression is at least twice as common among cohabitors as it is among married partners," says professor Jan Stets, based on her research into cohabitation and violence. Stets found that nearly 14 percent of cohabitors admit to hitting, shoving, or throwing things at their partner in the past year, compared to only 5 percent of married people. This rate held true even when controlling for factors as education, age, occupation, and income.[9]

Some attempt to explain away the higher rates of domestic violence in cohabiting relationships by saying married women are less likely to report violence against them. But that is an unfounded assumption. Married women are more likely to have helpful and caring networks of friends and family, while cohabitors more often report feeling isolated. Also, those who raise this objection do not understand how this research is done. The best studies control for such factors—and still show significantly higher levels of violence among cohabitors.

Linda Waite, a sociologist from the University of Chicago, found that in marriages the male-to-female ratio of violence is balanced—women are just as likely to initiate violence against their spouse as men. But in cohabiting relationships, she found not only does the rate of violence increase but the ratio also becomes imbalanced—with men more likely to initiate violence.[10] Additionally, Canadian and US studies both found that women in cohabiting relationships are about nine times more likely to be killed by their live-in partner than are women who are married to their partners.[11]

As one scholar concludes in the *Journal of Family Violence*, "Regardless of methodology . . . cohabitors engage in more violence than spouses."[12]

Men with rings on their fingers appear to be very different kinds of men. Safer men.

A CHEATING HEART

Most couples, married or not, expect sexual faithfulness for themselves and their partner. How many folks do you know who are happy for their partner to seek out extracurricular sex partners? But the type of relationship they live in is a strong indicator whether their wishes for sexual fidelity are realized. The ring makes a difference.

Numerous studies consistently show that cohabitors have much higher levels of sexual infidelity than married couples.[13] According to research done at the University of California-Irvine, "The odds of a recent infidelity were more than twice as high for cohabitors than for married persons." This held true even when researchers controlled for issues such as permissive values about extramarital sexuality. They concluded that the "commitment mechanisms" of marriage were the likely reasons for the difference.[14]

The highly reputable National Sex Survey found an even greater divide, reporting that live-in boyfriends are nearly *four times* more likely than husbands to cheat in the past year. And while women are generally more faithful, cohabiting women are *eight times* more likely than wives to cheat.[15] It seems that if you want to give someone the experience of sexual opportunism with other partners, cohabitation is what you are looking for. But if a faithful partner is your desire, then cohabitation is not your thing.

Other researchers found that the levels of sexual exclusivity among cohabitors were more on par with single, dating couples.[16] A study published in the *Journal of Marriage and Family* explains that "cohabiting women are more similar to dating women than they are to married women" and "cohabitation before marriage is still associated with reduced sexual exclusivity *after* marriage" (emphasis added).[17] As we will see, cohabitors more closely resemble singles than married people in a number of other important behaviors and attitudes.

Researchers conclude that the commitment and relational clarity of marriage—the couple as well as their friends and family having a clearer understanding of the nature of the relationship—served to protect against infidelity. This affects not only both people in the relationship but also potential outside sexual partners. A man or woman with a wedding ring is more off-limits than someone without a ring. We have names for people who disregard these powerful symbols. The same is not true for those who are merely cohabiting. Have you ever heard anyone say with shock, "You slept with a cohabiting woman (or man)?"

EARNING AND SAVING MONEY

Most of us have concerns about money. Will we be able to earn enough to pay our bills? Will we lose our job? What if we can't save enough for the future? Often our financial strength (or weakness) determines our future. It is no small thing. Does the nature of our relationship with our partner have any impact on our financial well-being?

Research over the past few decades consistently finds that marriage is a wealth-building institution. Married people typically earn and save more than their unmarried counterparts—cohabiting or single.[18]

How can this be? If Leon and Leona have the same level of education and general employability as Frank and Francine—but the only difference is Leon and Leona are married while Frank and Francine are living together—how could this make a difference in their income and savings? Common sense would indicate that a dual-earning household would be likely to make and keep more money, regardless whether the two earners have a marriage license, right?

What could marital status possibly have to do with financial smarts?

But this is exactly what the best science is showing. It is not just the joining of resources and energies that creates this financial benefit but the permanence and dependability of marriage that enhances that process. This is seen time and again.

Research from Purdue University finds that wealth accumulation in cohabiting situations is far below what is typical in marriage, with cohabitors—again—more closely resembling the earnings and savings rates of singles.[19] The National Marriage Project reports that while the poverty rate for children living in married households is about 6 percent, it jumps to 31 percent for children with a cohabiting mother and father—much closer to the 45 percent rate for children in single parent families.[20]

And while there might be the possibility of two earners in a cohabiting relationship, these informal partners experience less sharing and pooling of resources than married couples.[21] This can reduce the very real "two can live as cheaply as one" factor when the two are living more as a set of distinct *ones*.

Cohabitors act financially more like roommates than a team, as married couples do. In fact, very recent research shows that among low- and moderate-income people, married couples were more likely to be able to buy a home—and to do so faster—than cohabiting couples. The researchers found the "stability and commitment" of marriage is what boosted a couple's increased ability to purchase a home.[22]

CLEANING THE TOILET

One of the nice things about being in a domestic relationship has nothing to do with the bedroom. It has to do with the bathroom . . . and the kitchen and vacuum cleaners. You have someone to share the chores of keeping a house clean. Contrary to stereotypes, married men are more likely to help out with a variety of household chores than men who are just living with their girlfriend. A man with a ring on his finger will spend up to eight more hours a week washing dishes and cleaning clothes, floors, and bathrooms than his shacking-up peer. Ladies, do you hear that?

A MAN with a ring

on his finger will spend up to

eight more hours a week

washing dishes and cleaning clothes,

floors, and bathrooms

than his shacking-up peer.

A man's educational status also increases his likelihood of helping around the house—but not as much as marriage does.[23] And to make all this better, the man with the ringed finger is less likely to object to doing these extra chores as his un-ringed peers. That is good news for men, women, and our nation's toilets. Bad news for dust bunnies.

HIGH-RISK BEHAVIOR

Why do you think that life insurance and auto insurance policies cost less if you are married—because of strict morality and an adherence to traditions? When your insurance agent is writing your policy and charges you more for *not* being married, ask if it makes any difference that you are cohabiting. What do you think the answer will be? What if you explain that cohabiting is just *like* being married? Their actuary tables are not determined by morality, sentimentality, or traditionalism but by careful, reliable research. The whole idea of insurance relies on such exact and informed measures. And insurance companies find that rings make a big, practical difference.

"During their twenties, young men and women who lived together showed very high and increasing rates of health-destroying and danger-ous behaviors," Linda Waite and Maggie Gallagher conclude from their exhaustive research into the differences between married and cohabiting households.[24] These behaviors include heavier levels of smoking, drink-ing, wild carousing, and even illegal drug use.

Married men and women are consistently less careless and accident-prone than their single and cohabiting peers. And men who are married are not as likely to be out late at bars, driving their cars and motorcycles too fast, or taking chances at dangerous pursuits.

Research also found that married women were far less likely to be attacked by a stranger than single or cohabiting women. But how does an assailant know the marital status of a particular female victim? They don't check ring fingers before they attack. It's because married women are not as likely to be out in dark, isolated parking lots late at night. Their husbands are more protective and make sure they don't go out alone late at night.

COMMITMENT VS. TOGETHERNESS

Given the findings of the scientific literature, sociologists conclude, "It is difficult to argue that cohabiters resemble married people."[25]

"Studies reveal a consistently and significantly lower level of relational satisfaction among cohabiting couples than among married couples," says professor Bruce Wydick, an economist studying family dynamics at the University of San Francisco. From his sophisticated investigations, he concludes, "It appears to be *commitment* rather than mere *togetherness* that lays the foundation for long-term cooperation and happiness in family relationships"[26] (emphasis in original).

Marriage provides that essential commitment in ways that cohabitation simply does not and cannot. It binds the couple in important and measurably beneficial ways.

And cohabitors look more like singles in nearly all the important measures of well-being, rather than looking like those couples who can show you their rings and marriage license.

"Scholars increasingly regard cohabitation as a substitute to being single, not an alternative to marriage," notes James Q. Wilson.[27] Other studies confirm that cohabitation is closer to singleness than to marriage in terms of contributing to well-being outcomes.[28] The key factor is not just that there are two but *how* the two are joined.

This is because marriage is a fundamentally different kind of relationship. Cohabitation is not only more ambiguous for the couple—with men and women often holding differing opinions about the seriousness and future of the relationship—but also for their friends and extended family.[29]

No one is quite sure about the relationship. Her father wonders if the young man is really serious about his daughter. Is he in it for the long haul—or is he likely to be gone in six months? His mother wants to know if this relationship is durable enough to provide her first grandchild. Is this woman really committed to her son? Is their relationship headed toward marriage, or are they just seeing what happens? How would the guy answer that? Would his answer be different than the woman's? Cohabitation—by definition—keeps everyone wondering. And sometimes wondering constantly. As scholars have called it, cohabitation is the oxymoron of an "ambiguous commitment."[30]

Marriage, however, makes a clear statement—not only between the couple but also to the larger community—about where these two stand with one another. The wedding makes a dramatic, conclusive statement—like the one the Spanish conqueror Cortez made in destroying his fleet after landing on the shores of Mexico. He was saying to himself and to all, as the bride and groom say to each other and their family and friends upon landing on the new shore of marriage:

I'm here. This is the place I have been seeking all my life! And I am not going back. I can't go back! There is no "back." Building my life here in this place, with these people is my destiny.

Cortez realized the absoluteness of his actions. He was sending a clear message of his absolute intentions to any of his men who had thoughts of retreat. His commitment was clear to all. It was total. And it made a difference in how he approached his new life. He was not halfhearted or double-minded. He was in it for the long haul, having closed his only escape route.

Such is the commitment made by the married. It makes a profound difference in the nature of their relationship. Marriage is not just sentimental. Husbands and wives are much different people—in a very different kind of relationship—than their cohabiting peers. This is why the data on the outcomes of these two types of relationships is so stark. We will learn more about how different they are in the coming chapters.

Which kind of relationship do you think is more likely to make you happy and content? Which do you think will produce more positive, healthy outcomes? You don't have to take a wild, hopeful guess at the answer.

QUESTIONS
for Couples

1. What were some of the findings you found surprising about the differing outcomes researchers have found among marrieds and cohabitors?

2. How can you imagine marriage affecting these factors in a couple's lives? How could the clarity of commitment in a marriage have this sort of impact?

3. Based on what you learned in this chapter, what would be your advice to a younger couple who is considering cohabiting?

RECOMMENDED RESOURCES

Glenn T. Stanton, *Why Marriage Matters: Reasons to Believe in Marriage in Postmodern Society* (Colorado Springs: NavPress, 1997).

Susan L. Brown and Alan Booth, "Cohabitation versus Marriage: A Comparison of Relational Quality," *Journal of Marriage and Family* 58 (1996): 668–78.

Linda J. Waite and Maggie Gallagher, *The Case for Marriage: Why Married People Are Happier, Healthier, and Better Off Financially* (New York: Doubleday, 2000).

Bruce Wydick, "Grandma Was Right: Why Cohabitation Undermines Relational Satisfaction, but Is Increasing Anyway," *Kyklos* 60 (2007): 617–45.

NOTES

1. James Q. Wilson, *The Marriage Problem: How Our Culture Has Weakened Families* (New York: Harper Collins, 2002), 38.

2. Arland Thornton, William G. Axinn, and Yu Xie, *Marriage and Cohabitation* (Chicago: University of Chicago Press, 2007), 83–84.

3. Michael D. Newcomb and P. M. Bentler, "Assessment of Personality and Demographic Aspects of Cohabitation and Marital Success," *Journal of Personality Assessment* 44 (1980): 11–24.

4. Jan E. Stets, "The Link between Past and Present Intimate Relationships," *Journal of Family Issues* 14 (1993): 236–60.

5. Susan L. Brown and Alan Booth, "Cohabitation versus Marriage: A Comparison of Relational Quality," *Journal of Marriage and Family* 58 (1996): 668–78.

6. Thornton et al., 2007, 82.

7. Kersti Yllo and Murray A. Straus, "Interpersonal Violence among Married and Cohabiting Couples," *Family Relations* 30 (1981): 339–47.

8. Albert R. Roberts, "Psychological Characteristics of Batterers: A Study of 234 Men Charged with Domestic Violence Offenses," *Journal of Family Violence* 2 (1987): 81–93.

9. Jan E. Stets, "Cohabiting and Marital Aggression: The Role of Social Isolation," *Journal of Marriage and Family* 53 (1991): 669–80.

10. Linda J. Waite, "Trends in Men's and Women's Well-Being on Marriage," in *The Ties That Bind: Perspectives on Marriage and Cohabitation*, ed. Linda J. Waite (New York: Walter de Gruyter, 2000), 382.

11. Todd K. Shackelford, "Cohabitation, Marriage and Murder," *Aggressive Behavior* 27 (2001): 284–91; Margo Wilson, M. Daly, and C. Wright, "Uxoricide in Canada: Demographic Risk Pattern," *Canadian Journal of Criminology* 35 (1993): 263–91.

12. Nicky Ali Jackson, "Observational Experiences of Intrapersonal Conflict and Teenage Victimization: A Comparative Study among Spouses and Cohabitors," *Journal of Family Violence* 11 (1996): 191–203.

13. John D. Cunningham and John K. Antill, "Cohabitation and Marriage: Retrospective and Predictive Comparisons," *Journal of Social and Personal Relationships* 11 (1994): 77–94.

14. Judith Treas and Deirdre Giesen, "Sexual Fidelity among Married and Cohabiting Americans," *Journal of Marriage and Family* 62 (2000): 48–60.

15. Linda J. Waite and Maggie Gallagher, *The Case for Marriage: Why Married People Are Happier, Healthier, and Better Off Financially* (New York: Doubleday, 2000), 93.

16. Thornton et al., 2007, 82.

17. Renata Forste and Koray Tanfer, "Sexual Exclusivity among Dating, Cohabiting, and Married Women," *Journal of Marriage and Family* 58 (1996): 33–47.

18. Waite and Gallagher, 2000, 110–23.

19. Janet Wilmoth and Gregor Koso, "Does Marital History Matter? Marital Status and Wealth Outcomes among Preretirement Adults," *Journal of Marriage and Family* 64 (2002): 254–68.

20. David Popenoe and Barbara Dafoe Whitehead, "Should We Live Together? What Young Adults Need to Know about Cohabitation before Marriage," *The National Marriage Project,* Rutgers University, 2002, 9.

21. Thornton et al., 2007, 83; Wilson, 2002, 39.

22. Michal Grinstein-Weiss et al., "The Effect of Marital Status on Homeownership among Low-Income Households," Working Paper Series WP-10-06, *National Center for Family & Marriage Research*, Bowling Green State University, June 2010, 22.

23. Teresa Ciabattari, "Cohabitation and Housework: The Effects of Marital Intentions," *Journal of Marriage and Family* 66 (2004): 118–25.

24. Waite and Gallagher, 2000, 63–64; Andrew J. Cherlin, *The Marriage-Go-Round: The State of Marriage and Family in America Today* (New York: Alfred A. Knopf, 2009), 100.

25. Frances Goldscheider, Arland Thornton, and Linda Young-DeMarco, "A Portrait of the Nest Leaving Process in Early Adulthood," *Demography* 30 (1993): 683–99.

26. Bruce Wydick, "Grandma Was Right: Why Cohabitation Undermines Relational Satisfaction, but Is Increasing Anyway," *Kyklos* 60 (2007): 617–45.

27. Wilson, 2002, 39.

28. Wendy D. Manning and Pamela J. Smock, "Measuring and Modeling Cohabitation: New Data from Qualitative Data," *Journal of Marriage and Family* 67 (2005): 989–1002.

29. Jo M. Lindsay, "An Ambiguous Commitment: Moving into a Cohabiting Relationship," *Journal of Family Studies* 6 (2000): 120–34; Scott M. Stanley, Galena K. Rhoades, and Sarah W. Whitton, "Commitment: Functions, Formation, and the Securing of Romantic Attachment," Journal of Family Theory & Review 2 (2010): 243–57.

30. Lindsay, 2000.

IF a couple wants to

increase to a near-certainty their

likelihood of divorcing once they do

marry, then live together before mar-

riage. And to improve dramatically

their chances of avoiding divorce, all

*they have to do is **not** do something.*

4

IS TEST-DRIVING
YOUR MARRIAGE SMART?

YOU'VE WORKED HARD, saved your money, and now you're ready. Today you take the plunge and buy that new laptop computer you've had your eye on. You've researched it thoroughly and you know it has all the features you want. There is only one thing left to do before handing the clerk your debit card. You want to try it out. You want to experience the brilliance of the graphics. You want to see how light it is and feel the action of the keyboard. How big does the screen really seem while watching a movie or playing a game?

You get to the store, tell the clerk which machine you are interested in—that you have largely made your decision to purchase—but there is one last thing you need to do. You want to try it out. Touch it. Use it. Get a feel for it.

She shakes her head. Unfortunately, that is not possible. This store requires you to commit to the purchase before you can try the product. Only then can you use it. Buy, then test.

Your friend does the same with a new car she's looking at. She knows what she wants: the model, color, and options—but the salesman won't let her test-drive the car until she has signed a contract and turned over a sizable down payment. "We find it's better to let people actually drive our cars only when we know they have a vested interested in caring for the car," the salesman says. "We find this only happens when people have made a commitment to purchase the car."

So no test-drive! Either you want it or you don't. Make up your mind.

How many computers or cars do you think these folks would sell with such a policy? Who in their right mind would make a big leap without trying it out first?

But don't we do the same with marriage? We ask young people to make one of the biggest commitments of their lives—rivaled only by their decision to become parents—without any prior experience of what marriage is actually like.

Marriage doesn't let you take it out of the box, unwrap it, and see how it works. Wouldn't it be smarter to try it first and see how it feels? Make sure it's right for you—and not just for you but also for the one who will be your spouse? And in a way, doesn't this approach actually take marriage more seriously than just jumping into it blind?

Isn't this the brilliance of cohabitation? A test-drive of something as serious as marriage—matrimony on training wheels. If things go poorly, then game off. Each goes their own way to healthier relationships and greater happiness. But if you like the feel of things and it's working, you can dive into the deeper waters of actual marriage with more assurance.

What about this doesn't make sense? It seems like a smart approach to building a healthy marriage, doesn't it?

NO LONG-TERM CONTRACT

Jean and Bill met on the job, both working for a retail store at a strip mall selling cell phones and PDAs. They quickly became very close, eventually spending most of their free time together. Bill would stay over at Jean's apartment on weekends, and soon he was sleeping at her place more often than at his.

They both knew their relationship was very serious. And given that one of their apartments was sitting vacant most nights, and that they both would like to build more of a life together, they decided to move more than Bill's toothbrush in with Jean's things.

This gave them both the opportunity to see if they were really compatible and experience what living as a married couple was really like. Would they get along? Would they find the other had quirks they just couldn't live with? Unlike their customers at work who are required to sign long-term contracts from the start, Bill and Jean believed their no-contract arrangement would enhance their relationship and prevent potential heartache.

This is precisely what millions of young couples in the past several decades have thought. Today, more than half of cohabiting couples see their live-in arrangement as exactly that: a test-drive of the relationships before marriage.[1]

You no longer have to *wonder* if this is a good idea. You can *know!* A great deal of careful and sophisticated social science research has scrutinized the experiences of the growing number of couples who assume premarital cohabitation is a smart testing ground for marriage. Sociologists and psychologists at leading universities have been very interested to learn if cohabiting is an effective testing ground for marriage. Does living together before the wedding lead to healthier, happier, and longer marriages?

Let's look at what these scholars have learned.

As we saw in the previous chapter, cohabiting relationships, compared to those of their married peers, tend to be significantly less healthy. They tend to be plagued by higher levels of sexual infidelity, are more violent and emotionally volatile, and are much shorter-lasting.

TESTING THE TESTING GROUND

But does the experience of cohabiting teach couples things that help make them better spouses once they do marry?

Unfortunately, it does not. Not even close!

This is a rare instance where there's a chasm the size of the Grand Canyon between what many young adults believe about relationships and the proven reality of their experience. And it is not the moralizing preachers and traditionalists saying so. The robust, diverse, and conclusive scientific research on this question leaves no doubt about whether cohabiting is helpful to marriage. Graduate and postdoctoral seminars in sociology are held on this topic, and this is what they learn.

Higher Divorce Rates

Sociologists investigating this question—working from two leading schools of sociology, the Universities of Chicago and Michigan—tell us clearly that the:

> expectation of a positive relationship between cohabitation and marital stability . . . has been shattered in recent years by studies conducted in several Western countries, including Canada, Sweden, New Zealand, and the United States.

Their data indicates that people with cohabiting experience who marry have a 50 to 80 percent higher likelihood of divorcing than married couples who never cohabited.[2] A Canadian sociologist explains:

> Contrary to conventional wisdom that living together before marriage will screen out poor matches and therefore improve subsequent marital stability, there is considerable empirical evidence demonstrating that premarital cohabitation is associated with lowered marital stability.[3]

After surveying the data on this question, another leading scholar contends that the only conclusion one could honestly reach was to categorically "reject the argument" that cohabitation contributes to stronger marriages.[4]

PEOPLE with cohabiting experience

who marry have a 50 to 80 percent higher

likelihood of divorcing than

married couples who never cohabited.

"Marriages that are preceded by living together have 50 percent higher disruption rates than marriages without premarital cohabitation," said noted demographer Larry Bumpass from the University of Wisconsin-Madison and sociologist Andrew Cherlin of Johns Hopkins.[5]

Impaired Relationships

An early investigation from UCLA looked at the actual quality of marriages preceded by cohabitation—not just the longevity. They found serious differences in relational quality between those who cohabited prior to marriage and those who did not.

> In regard to problem areas, it was found that cohabitors experienced significantly more difficulty in their marriages with adultery, alcohol, drugs and independence than couples who did not cohabit. Apparently, this makes marriage preceded by cohabitation more prone to problems often associated with other deviant lifestyles—for example, use of drugs and alcohol, more permissive sexual relationships and an abhorrence of dependence—than marriages not preceded by cohabitation.[6]

Show of hands—who wants more of those things in their marriage? The dependence/independence aspect of marriage is important because healthy relationships are built by two healthy individuals learning to rely on one another—each having the confidence and security that they have someone to depend on in life's trials. This is particularly important as children come along and the couple's financial, emotional, and day-to-day responsibilities increase.

And as their children grow, they will learn lessons from their parents about how to act in healthy ways in their relationships. So there are important intergenerational factors here. These things matter more than young couples might yet imagine.

Research is also discovering the process of cohabiting itself can influence couples to learn to communicate, negotiate, and settle differences in ways that are less healthy and honest than those of couples who didn't cohabit before marriage. This is probably because without a clearly defined relationship, the cohabiting couple can learn to be more con-trolling and manipulative with each other. And this leads to relational resentment and mistrust.

THE COHABITATION EFFECT

This conclusion by sociologists that premarital cohabitation dramati-cally increases the risk of divorce, as well as the overall unhealthiness of the relationships, has become so consistent, it has been given a name: *the cohabitation effect.* When scholars and students of the family use that term, they all know what is meant, and you can find many studies inves-tigating the reasons for this effect. The scholars no longer debate *whether* there is a tight connection between premarital cohabitation and marital divorce but rather *why* there is a connection.

Let's continue examining the research on this.

Doctors Claire Kamp-Dush and her professor Paul Amato conducted a unique investigation that tracked two groups of cohabitors who even-tually married: one who married between 1964 and 1980 and another who did so between 1981 and 1997. This allowed them to see if there were any changes in the cohabitation effect as cohabitation became more common and more accepted by society. An important angle to study.

But they found "there was little evidence that the negative conse-quences of cohabitation dissipated over time as cohabitation became more prevalent." Even after controlling for various social and economic factors that could account for such a difference, they discovered premarital cohab-itors in both groups were significantly more likely to have lower levels of marital happiness, more marital conflict, and higher levels of divorce.[7]

This indicates that the cohabitation effect appears to have more to do with the process of cohabitation itself—not society's acceptance or rejec-tion of it and the pressure this might put on cohabiting couples.

"One of the most clearly defined correlates of cohabitation is an increased risk of marital dissolution," says professor Jay Teachman of Western Washington University. In a more recent examination of cohabi-tation's impact on marital success, he notes that cohabitation increases the possibility of divorce by as much as 50 percent. He even calls cohabitation one of the most "robust predictors of marital dissolution"—making living together first one of the *worst* things you can do for your marriage. Teachman also warns that even premarital sex by itself is associated with an increased risk of marital disruption, though at lower rates than living together before marriage.[8] In both situations (premarital sex and cohabitation) intimate emotional, physical, and even spiritual bonds are being made—without being backed up by the kind of commitment they demand. It is like walking on a tightrope without a net below.

INTIMATE emotional, physical,

and even spiritual bonds are being made—

without being backed up by the kind

of commitment they demand. It is like

walking on a tightrope without a net below.

Marriage, however, is like walking on firm ground. You might occasionally stumble, but the consequences of that stumble are dramatically lessened. Because of the total commitment of the relationship itself, there is a greater feeling of security. This is another reason married people consistently report being more satisfied with their sexual lives, both physically and emotionally, than couples who are dating or cohabiting.[9] Marriage provides the security, closeness, trust, and long-term intimacy that allows a couple's sexual passion, comfort, expertise, and joy to develop and thrive.

A 2010 meta-analysis looked at twenty-six peer-reviewed, published studies that followed various couples over time. This analysis found that marrieds who had cohabiting pasts were more likely to face divorce, and that "noncohabitors seem to have more confidence in the future of their relationship, and have less accepting attitudes toward divorce."

And as with other studies, the married couples with no cohabiting past are less likely to engage in aggressive and negative interactions, experience more overtly positive interactions, and enjoy more positive communications.[10] These researchers conclude, based on their review of the best studies to date:

> The major practical implication of this review is that psychologists can inform the public, that despite popular belief, cohabitation is generally associated with negative outcomes both in terms of marital quality and marital stability . . .

The numbers vary, from 50 to 80 percent, on how significantly cohabitation increases a marriage's chance of failure. Clearly, the numbers are consistently very high—too high for any couples to take comfort from.

But the average marriage preceded by cohabitation faces a 65 percent *greater* likelihood of divorce.[11] And marriages not preceded by cohabitation have a risk of divorce *well below* the 40 percent divorce likelihood for the average couple.

In fact, if a couple wants to *increase* to a near certainty their likelihood of divorcing once they do marry, there are few things more widely practiced that could accomplish this more efficiently than living together before marriage. And just think, all they have to do is *not* do this and they can dramatically improve their chances of avoiding divorce. How difficult is that?

Other studies report that marriages where only one spouse had cohabited also face a 50 percent increased risk of divorce.[12] Another study finds, "Over 50% of cohabiting unions in the US, whether or not they are eventually legalized by marriage, end by separation within five years compared to roughly 20% for marriages" with no history of cohabitation.[13] Cohabiting relationships are five times more likely to dissolve than married relationships (even when children are involved), and when separated, cohabitors are only 33 percent as likely to reconcile.[14]

And cohabitors who live with a few different partners, then finally marry, face *double the odds of divorce* of those who cohabited only with their spouse.[15]

Is test-driving a potential marriage smart? Professors Scott Stanley and Galena K. Rhoades—two groundbreaking scholars in this area of study—put the matter succinctly: The belief that cohabiting prior to marriage lowers one's odds of divorce has no evidence going for it, yet it is a strongly held belief.[16]

In fact, it is difficult to find another belief about relationships that is so widely held, but lacking any actual support.

WHY THE COHABITATION EFFECT?

What makes cohabitors more likely to face increased troubles in their relationships and their marriages—and dramatically increase their odds of divorce?

Reason #1—Lack of Commitment

Research over the past two decades has come to reliable conclusions about why cohabitation brings a greater risk of divorce. A key answer centers on commitment. As we learned in the previous chapter, one sophisticated study on relationship dynamics concludes that "it appears to be *commitment* rather than mere *togetherness* that lays the foundation for long-term cooperation and happiness in family relationships."[17] Cohabitors are shown to be consistently less committed to both their relationship and their partner.[18] But all is not equal between the sexes when it comes to who consistently has the lower commitment. (We will look at this more closely in chapter 7.) Care to guess whether that's the guy or the gal? *It's primarily the guy.*

Scott Stanley and Howard Markman, leaders in the field, explain that:

Men who cohabit with their wives are, on average, a good deal less dedicated to their wives *even once they are married!* It is quite notable that this difference was not observed at all in females. (emphasis in original)

They warn: "Practically, the data hint at the importance of women giving particular consideration to the interpersonal commitment levels of the men they are dating, living with, or marrying."[19]

Commitment—having the couple as well as their friends and families understand the clear and public promise of marriage—makes a significant difference in relational health and longevity. Every important party to the relationship is clear on where the relationship stands. This is what the wedding is about—why it takes place in front of all the couple's important friends and family members, why there are pictures taken, why there is a celebration of the event, and why they keep a record of this public commitment at City Hall. Everyone witnessed the fact. They heard the vows. They understand the promises made. If the couple later announces to their friends, their family, the wedding officiate, and the clerk at City Hall that they have changed their minds about their vows and just want to call the whole thing off, they will be in for a big surprise.

This is marriage. It provides safety and security for the relationship. It is more than just a decision the couple makes, then decides they can unmake. Cohabitation is different. University of Virginia sociologist Steven Nock famously described cohabitation as "an incomplete institution suffused with ambiguity."[20] He was precisely right.

Living together means something different to everyone, based on what the partners and their families are most recently told. When asked where the relationship was leading, more women than men in cohabiting relationships are likely to say it is eventually leading to marriage.

"Are Rick and Melinda getting married?" a friend of Melinda's mom asks.

She responds, "Rick says as soon as he finishes school they will start making plans."

That's all they have to go on—and perhaps Melinda has more hope in that promise than Rick, her mother . . . or her mother's friends.

Everyone knows where a married couple stands with one another—most importantly the couple and both sets of in-laws. Not so with cohabitors.

Reason #2—Cohabitation Teaches Unhealthy Relationship Skills

Couples who cohabit before marriage tend to exhibit more negative and less successful problem-solving skills than married couples. They are also less likely to show supportive and self-sacrificing attitudes and behaviors. Scholars find this is due to the nature of cohabiting relationships. The lack of commitment can train the couple to interact and negotiate in less healthy and honest ways.[21]

This is because the lack of relational clarity is likely to foster more controlling and manipulative interactions to try to keep the relationship together and get the partner to do what the other desires. As a result, cohabitors are much more likely to report a sense of relational instability than their married peers.[22]

When people who first cohabit do marry, they bring these problem behaviors and attitudes into their marriage, putting them at risk for poor communication. Researchers from Penn State, another university with a world-class sociology of family department, explain:

> The results involving problem solving behavior suggest premarital cohabitation is associated with more destructive and divisive communication behaviors during marriage that are less likely to achieve a successful resolution, and may in turn, contribute to marital deterioration over time.[23]

This same research shows that spouses who cohabit before marriage are less effective in soliciting support from their mate and less likely to be able to provide it themselves—not a positive combination in building a healthy relationship. This ability to seek and provide social, emotional, and spiritual support is fundamental to any relationship. But it appears that cohabitors learn to do this less effectively, whether or not they eventually marry.

COHABITATION is really

an insult to your beloved:

"I'm not totally sure about you.

Can I give you a test-drive first,

so I can be sure?"

This study also observed that the relational ambiguity of just living together is more likely to lead to a sense of *"permanent availability,"* which is "being perpetually in the market for a more attractive partner regardless of relationship status."[24] Few of us want our partners to feel they are still in the market, sexually and relationally. This can help explain why infidelity is consistently so much higher among cohabitors, as we saw earlier.

Cohabitors are more likely to feel they have at least one eye, if not a foot, still in the relational and sexual marketplace. And while this might be true of some marrieds, it is not close to how true it is for too many cohabitors.

WHICH TYPES ARE MOST HARMFUL?

Serial cohabitation—living with a succession of partners before marriage—increases one's likelihood of relational difficulty and later divorce even beyond the very high levels of those who cohabit only once.

But as the body of evidence about cohabitation grows, recent research is finding one form of cohabitation that does not produce the full array of negative results and as great a risk of divorce. It is important to understand what sets this form apart, but also how it remains consistent with what we have learned about cohabiting relationships.

Couples who cohabit before their engagement "show the highest risk for relationship distress before marriage and that this risk is not likely to diminish after marriage."[25] But what about couples who cohabit between the formal engagement and the wedding? Studies are finding that while this type of cohabitation is associated with poorer relationship interactions (both before and after the wedding), it is not nearly as harmful—in terms of personal and relational well-being—as pre-engagement and serial cohabitation.[26]

This is important to note, not as a green light for engaged couples to cohabit but to understand why there is a practical difference. It is what we have already learned. I call it the "mothers-in-law have ordered their dresses" factor. And it matters. Let me explain.

As we know, cohabitation carries no commitment or promise. It is, by definition, ambiguous. While engagement is not marriage, it's more than nothing. It's a promise, or at least an agreed-upon intention, which is not only well-known to the couple but also to their circle of family and friends.

And this makes a big difference in how the couple and those around them understand the relationship and act toward it.

A man and woman with a wedding date set, invitations and her dress ordered, and a wedding hall reserved—not to mention two mothers-in-law giddy about the big day and making plans for their own dresses—will behave more like a married couple, in terms of commitment and selflessness, when compared with other cohabitors. Both sets of in-laws are willing to shell out some money to help with security deposits for wedding preparations. Plans are being made. Commitments have been announced. This matters in very practical ways. There is greater relational clarity.

But at the same time, they don't completely resemble the dynamics of married folks. The big promise and commitment have still not been fully made. Engagements have been known to end before the marriage. Such an event will put that once-engaged, cohabiting couple in the group of people who cohabited with someone other than their spouse.

A man and a woman are not husband and wife until the preacher or judge announces them as such. Until the fat lady sings! But this finding regarding post-engagement cohabitation does align with the earlier finding that it is *commitment*, or the lack of it, that makes most cohabiting relationships dicey.

A SPOUSE IS NOT A CONSUMER PRODUCT

Young couples interested in forming a thriving, healthy, and lifelong marriage—and that includes most of us—should understand that the wisdom of trying something first applies only to products that you buy: computers, cars, and clothing. Thinking it applies to marriage is pure make-believe, like Sasquatch, mermaids, and unicorns.

You are not buying a husband or a wife. Your potential spouse is not a consumer product. The wedding chapel is not Sears, where they guarantee satisfaction or your money back. You are committing your life to someone, to care for them, to love them, to give yourself totally, for better or for worse. Either you are up for it or you are not.

In fact, cohabitation is really an insult to your beloved: "I'm not totally

sure about you. Can I give you a test-drive first, so I can be sure?" Melts
your heart, doesn't it?

Seldom is something believed so widely, but lacking any shred of evidence, than the belief that living together before marriage makes for better
relationships. As we saw in this chapter, there is *nothing* so many couples
do at their own hand, by their own consent, to so seriously harm their
future marital prospects than to live together before marrying.

Carlos, a man in his late twenties living and working in San Diego,
saw his marriage of three years die last year. He lived with his first serious
girlfriend for seven months before that relationship ended. Then he
moved in with the woman who would become his wife. They cohabited
for two and a half years before their wedding. He explains in common,
honest language what scholars express in academic prose:

> *My marriage failed 'cause I failed. I learned from my early relation-
> ships how to treat a woman in ways she don't ever want to be treated.
> I thought it was all about me and that ain't no way to keep a marriage.*

He says he wishes he would have learned better, but cohabitation provided the wrong kind of education.

QUESTIONS
for Couples

I. Why do you think couples believe that cohabiting can boost their
chances of succeeding in marriage?

2. From what you have learned about cohabiting relationships, why
do you think researchers are finding that living together tends to
harm future marriages?

3. How do you think this might be true of you and your relationships?

4. How does the information in this chapter correspond with what
you have seen in friends and family members who have been in
cohabiting relationships?

5. Based on what you have learned, what would you advise a close friend who was considering living with their partner before marriage? If that situation were reversed, what would you want your friend to say to you?

RECOMMENDED RESOURCES

Jay Teachman, "Premarital Sex, Premarital Cohabitation and the Risk of Subsequent Marital Dissolution among Women," *Journal of Marriage and Family* 65 (2003): 444–55.

Anita Jose, K. Daniel O'Leary, and Anne Moyer, "Does Premarital Cohabitation Predict Subsequent Marital Stability and Marital Quality? A Meta-Analysis," *Journal of Marriage and Family* 72 (2010): 105–16.

Wendy Manning, Pamela Smock, and Debarun Majumdar, "The Relative Stability of Cohabiting and Marital Unions for Children," *Population Research and Policy Review* 23 (2004): 135–59.

Daniel Lichter and Zhenchao Qian, "Serial Cohabitation and the Marital Life Course," *Journal of Marriage and Family*, 70 (2008): 861–78.

Judith P. M. Soons and Matthijs Kalmijm, "Is Marriage More than Cohabitation? Well-Being Differences in 30 European Countries," *Journal of Marriage and Family* 71 (2009): 1141–57.

Laura Stafford, Susan L. Kline, and Caroline T. Rankin, "Married Individuals, Cohabitors, and Cohabitors Who Marry: A Longitudinal Study of Relational and Individual Well-Being," *Journal of Social and Personal Relationships* 21 (2004): 231–48.

NOTES

1. Arland Thornton et al., *Marriage and Cohabitation* (Chicago: University of Chicago Press, 2007), 87.

2. William G. Axinn and Arland Thornton, "The Relationship between Cohabitation and Divorce: Selectivity or Casual Influence?" *Demography* 29 (1992): 357–74.

3. Zheng Wu, "Premarital Cohabitation and Postmarital Cohabiting Union Formation," *Journal of Family Issues* 16 (1995): 212–32.

4. Alan Booth and David Johnson, "Premarital Cohabitation and Marital Success," *Journal of Family Issues* 9 (1988): 255–72.

5. Larry Bumpass, James A. Sweet, and Andrew Cherlin, "The Role of Cohabitation in Declining Rates of Marriage," *Journal of Marriage and Family* 53 (1991): 913–27.

6. Michael D. Newcomb and P. M. Bentler, "Assessment of Personality and Demographic Aspects of Cohabitation and Marital Success," *Journal of Personality Assessment* 44 (1980): 11–24.

7. Claire Kamp-Dush, Catherine L. Cohan, and Paul R. Amato, "The Relationship between Cohabitation and Marital Quality and Stability: Change across Cohorts?" *Journal of Marriage and Family* 65 (2003): 539–49.

8. Jay Teachman, "Premarital Sex, Premarital Cohabitation and the Risk of Subsequent Marital Dissolution among Women," *Journal of Marriage and Family* 65 (2003): 444–55.

9. Robert T. Michael et al., *Sex in America: A Definitive Survey*, 1994, 124–29; Edward O. Laumann et al., *The Social Organization of Sexuality: Sexual Practices in the United States*, 1994, 364, table 10.5; Andrew Greeley, *Faithful Attraction: Discovering Intimacy, Love and Fidelity in American Marriage*, St. Martin's, 1991, see chapter 6.

10. Anita Jose, K. Daniel O'Leary, and Anne Moyer, "Does Premarital Cohabitation Predict Subsequent Marital Stability and Marital Quality? A Meta-Analysis," *Journal of Marriage and Family* 72 (2010): 105–16.

11. Georgina Binstock and Arland Thornton, "Separations, Reconciliations, and Living Apart in Cohabiting and Marital Unions," *Journal of Marriage and Family* 65 (2003): 432–43, 441.

12. Susan Brown and Alan Booth, "Cohabitation versus Marriage: A Comparison of Relationship Quality," *Journal of Marriage and Family* 58 (1996): 668–78, 669.

13. Wendy Manning, Pamela Smock, and Debarun Majumdar, "The Relative Stability of Cohabiting and Marital Unions for Children," *Population Research and Policy Review* 23 (2004): 135–59, 137.

14. Binstock and Thornton, 2003, 440.

15. Daniel Lichter and Zhenchao Qian, "Serial Cohabitation and the Marital Life Course," *Journal of Marriage and Family* 70 (2008): 861–78, 874.

16. Scott M. Stanley and Galena K. Rhoades, "Sliding vs. Deciding: Understanding a Mystery," *Family Focus*, a newsletter of the National Council on Family Relations (Issue FF42), summer 2009, 1.

17. Bruce Wydick, "Grandma Was Right: Why Cohabitation Undermines Relational Satisfaction, but Is Increasing Anyway," *Kyklos* 60 (2007): 617–45, 642.

18. Judith P. M. Soons and Matthijs Kalmijm, "Is Marriage More than Cohabitation? Well-Being Differences in 30 European Countries," *Journal of Marriage and Family* 71 (2009):1141–57. They explain, "Relationship quality is lower than that of married unions, to a large extent, because cohabitants are less committed to their relationships . . . [and] moreover, married people invest more in their relationships and have a longer time horizon" (p. 1152); Scott M. Stanley, Sarah W. Whitton, and Howard J. Markman, "Maybe I Do: Interpersonal Commitment and Premarital or Nonmarital Cohabitation," *Journal of Family Issues* 25 (2004): 496–519.

19. Stanley et al., 2004, 512.

20. Steven L. Nock, "A Comparison of Marriages and Cohabiting Relationships," *Journal of Family Issues* 16 (1995): 53–76.

21. Laura Stafford, Susan L. Kline, and Caroline T. Rankin, "Married Individuals, Cohabitors, and Cohabitors Who Marry: A Longitudinal Study of Relational and Individual Well-Being," *Journal of Social and Personal Relationships* 21 (2004): 231–48.

22. Susan Brown, "The Effect of Union Type on Psychological Well-being: Depression among Cohabitors versus Marrieds," *Journal of Health and Social Behavior* 41 (2000): 241–55.

23. Catherine L. Cohan and Stacey Kleinbaum, "Toward a Greater Understanding of the Cohabitation Effect: Premarital Cohabitation and Marital Communication," *Journal of Marriage and Family* 64 (2002): 180–92.

24. Cohan et al., 2002, 190.

25. Galena Kline, Scott Stanley, Howard Markman et al., "Timing Is Everything: Pre-Engagement Cohabitation and Increased Risk for Poor Marital Outcomes," *Journal of Family Psychology* 18 (2004): 311–18.

26. Kline, Stanley, and Markman et al., 2004, 316.

CHILDREN are most likely

to thrive and live a happy life when

their mom and dad give them the life-

long gift of committing themselves to

one another in their marriage as well as

the extra effort and self-denial it takes

to make that marriage last and grow.

5

WHY MOM AND DAD'S MARRIAGE LICENSE MATTERS TO CHILDREN

LITTLE NICOLE—A RED-HAIRED, pigtailed, precociously spunky second-grader—lives with her mom and dad in Manhattan . . . Kansas. Pretty typical American kid. She loves school, her playmates, and her teacher. She says she wants to be a couple of things when she grows up: a singer, a dancer, a doctor, a pizza cook—"the kind with the big poofy hats"—a fireman . . . and a mom. She has all the drive in the world to become any or all of them. You can see it in her eyes. You can feel it in her spirit.

But she is young. She still has a great deal of growing to do. How will she be positioned in her developing years to accomplish her dreams? What kind of education will she get? Will her parents be able to afford good health care for her? Will they be able to live in a safe neighborhood? What kind of parents will they be? Will they be free from the struggles that hinder too many moms and dads from being the kinds of parents they should be: alcoholism, domestic violence, unemployment, outbursts of anger and emotional instability, and bouts with depression? These will all affect how far Nicole—like all children—gets in realizing her dreams, whether she achieves them or the new dreams she develops. We all know this.

But do we realize how much the relationship between her parents affects this? It's not just whether they get along. Not just if they are happy and on the job—but the very nature of their relationship. Are they married? Remarried? Are they both her parents or just one of them? Cohabiting? It matters—and it matters for children.

We usually think of cohabitation as involving only the couple—a man and woman trying to establish a life together. But this is shortsighted.

Few of us appreciate how many children figure into cohabitation's complicated relational equation. Of the more than 6.5 million cohabiting households in the United States, 41 percent have children living in them—up from 21 percent in 1987.[1] As the chart shows, the past few decades have seen a dramatic increase in the number of cohabiting households with one or more children.

What the chart doesn't show is the complexity of the relationships. Some of these children are living with both their mother and father. But many others are living with just one parent and that person's live-in partner. Seventy percent of children in cohabiting households are the child of only one of the partners.[2] Make note of this fact, for as we will see, this is cause for great concern.

Number of Cohabiting Homes with Children in the US

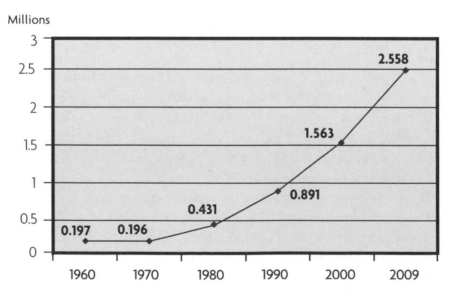

Across the United States, just over 40 percent of all children can expect to spend some part of their childhood or teen years in a cohabiting home.[3] That statistic is even higher in many other countries.

Gone are the days when cohabitation was a temporary setting for starry-eyed young people or college students in transition. This explosive growth of cohabiting homes with children means we must ask important questions:

- Does it really matter if the two people caring for children in a home are married?
- Are there any important differences between homes where mothers and fathers have rings on their fingers and those where they do not?
- What does this mean for real children like Nicole?

Given that a home, a community, or a nation's virtue can best be judged by how it cares for its children, this is a critical moral question.

We explore that question in this chapter.

The first point we must understand is the one I just asked you to take note of. When children live in a cohabiting home, they most likely live with only one biological parent—typically with Mom and her boyfriend. This makes a tremendous difference, given that children living in *married* step-homes—compared to children living with their own married mothers and fathers—face significantly increased levels of many important developmental problems.[4] It matters for children who the adults in their home actually are.

For a child to have an unrelated parenting-adult in the home, says eminent Rutgers family sociologist David Popenoe, is no small matter:

Social scientists used to believe that, for positive child outcomes, step-families were preferable to single-parent families. Today, we are not so sure. Stepfamilies typically have an economic advantage, but some recent studies indicate that the children of stepfamilies have as many behavioral and emotional problems as the children of single-parent families, and possibly more. . . . Stepfamily problems, in short, may be

so intractable that *the best strategy for dealing with them is to do everything possible to minimize their occurrence.*[5] (emphasis added)

A man coming into a new relationship will, more times than not, be
more interested in the woman than in her child. And many men will see her
child—even subconsciously—as a competitor for the time and attention he
seeks from the woman. This is true for married stepfathers—and even more
so for cohabiting "step"-fathers. Children have a sharp sense of who really
loves them . . . and who really does so when Momma is not around.

Here's how leading cohabitation scholar Susan L. Brown explains it:

Although cohabitation introduces a second adult to the household,
unless the partner is also the biological parent of the child, it is
unlikely that the partner's presence will raise the levels of warmth and
support to those of children in married families.

This is because "a cohabiting parent often occupies ambiguous family
roles characterized by little trust and authority, particularly from the
child's standpoint."[6] There's that word again: *ambiguous*. And Brown
asserts that even cohabitation itself can undermine the parenting effec-
tiveness of both adults in the home.

When children in a home belong to only one of the partners, according to a study of ten thousand individuals, the one who has the children
claims this situation "markedly increases the expectation of marriage and
decreases the expectation of never marrying." But this expectation is usually one-sided—not shared as seriously by the other partner, typically the
male. This increases the likelihood of arguments and tension, further low-
ering the expectation of marriage from the partner without children.[7]

No matter how cute children might be, we are not typically inclined
to make important investments in ones who are not our own. So a child
pays a price when he or she lives with a stepparent.

This is not to say that stepparents are not good people; many are
remarkably caring, loving parents. But scholars have explained that the
negative portrayal of stepparents in children's tales like Cinderella, Snow
White, and Hansel and Gretel has roots in reality. But where fairy tales

typically have an evil stepmother, in the real world it tends to be the live-in boyfriend who poses the real problems for children. This is because the biological connection—or the lack of it—matters in how adults treat children. And this factors into one of the most important dangers for children in their own homes: domestic violence.

SEXUAL AND PHYSICAL ABUSE OF CHILDREN

Will our little Nicole be victimized by either sexual or physical abuse? Much depends on the relational status of the adults in her home. And this is true whether the abuse may come from one of the adults in the home, a close family member or friend, or a complete stranger. Kids living with their two married parents are significantly less likely to become abuse victims. And children living in cohabiting situations are much more likely to become victims. We see this link in study after study, investigation after investigation. The most recent study conducted by the US government reports that a child living with mother and her boyfriend are around eleven times more likely to be emotionally, verbally, physically, and sexually abused compared to children living with their own *married* parents. And children living with their own cohabiting mother and father are four times more likely to be abused in all these ways compared to children living with their married mother and father. So both biology and marriage matter significantly for child safety in the home.[8] (However, children living with married adoptive mothers and fathers, of course, tend to be from very healthy and positive homes.)

"Children living with a caretaker other than two biological parents are at greater risk of child maltreatment," according to a special issue of the *Journal of Comparative Family Studies* that addressed family violence.[9] Children living with an adoptive, married mother and father are far less likely to face danger.

According to a study published in the journal *Pediatrics*, children residing in a home with a nonbiologically related adult were eight times more likely to *die* of maltreatment than children living with two biological parents.[10]

Consistent with other studies, their findings show the abuse most often comes from the mother's boyfriend. And his living in the home gives more access and opportunity to abuse the children. Although boyfriends provide a very small percentage of all nonparental child care, 64 percent of all nonparental abuse is committed by boyfriends. So leading researchers conclude, "A young child left with a mother's boyfriend experiences substantially elevated risk of abuse."[10]

"The evidence suggests that the most unsafe of all family environments for children is that in which the mother is living with someone other than the child's biological father," warn scholars at the National Marriage Project—a cooperative research and education effort now based at the University of Virginia.[12] Early published research reveals that "a number of studies have shown that girls living with non-natal fathers [boyfriends and stepfathers] are at higher risk for sexual abuse than girls living with natal fathers."[13] Given the serious and long-term emotional, psychological, and physical trauma created by such abuse, being cautious about cohabitation is not just moralizing. Children can live without a number of things and still thrive, but not without a safe environment.

POVERTY

The second most significant component for a child's well-being—because it drives so many other factors—is a family's ability to provide protection from poverty.

Again, a marriage license shared by a mother and father makes a significant difference. The general poverty rate for children with married parents is about 6 percent, while it is nearly 31 percent for children living with cohabiting parents. And 43 percent of these cohabiting parents have family incomes that place them in deep poverty.

Scholars examining child poverty in single-parent, cohabiting, and married homes repeatedly find that the socioeconomic status of children living with a cohabiting mother is closer to that of children living with a single parent than of children living with married parents. This happens even though *both* parents in cohabiting homes are *more likely* to be in the workforce than in married homes.[14]

Consider that. Cohabiting homes are more likely to have two paychecks coming in than married homes, but more likely to be living in poverty. This happens because marriage is shown to boost financial security, earning power, and savings. Just fifty years ago, the poverty level of children was determined primarily by their father's and mother's levels of employability. This is no longer true. Today, it is a result of the parents' marital status. As David Ellwood, Professor of Public Policy at Harvard University, notes:

> The vast majority of children who are raised entirely in a home where parents are married will never be poor during childhood. By contrast, the vast majority of children who spend time [in a home without their father] will experience poverty.[15]

To avoid family poverty, according to Professor Bill Galston, a former domestic policy adviser in the Clinton administration and now a senior fellow at the Brookings Institute, adults need to accomplish three primary goals:

1. Finish high school
2. Marry before having children
3. Marry after the age of twenty

Only 8 percent of families who do all three are poor—while 79 percent of those who fail to do these are poor.[16] Marriage breaks the vicious poverty cycle that traps generation after generation of children—and helps a couple generate more wealth in ways that cohabitation cannot.

Careful research also shows that marital status determines how parents spend the money they do have on their children. Cohabiting parents spend significantly less of their income on health care and education, but more on outside child care. They also spend substantially more on alcohol and tobacco for themselves compared with their married peers.

CHILDREN who live with

a mother and her unmarried partner

show significantly more problem behavior

both at home and at school.

This in turn prompts scholars to ask why a cohabiting family would "spend their money differently than [married or single] families with children, especially in terms of adult versus child-related goods?"[17]

One reason might be that—as we have seen in other family dynamics —cohabitors are more likely to watch out for themselves than for others. They haven't made the kind of commitment that compels us to want to sacrifice for others. This is what commitment does—but cohabitation doesn't call us to that. And children end up paying the price for it in many important ways that limit their healthy development.

ACADEMIC SUCCESS
AND PROBLEM BEHAVIOR

Kids like Nicole and her classmates who stay out of trouble are more likely to do better in school. Few teachers report that little troublemakers make good students. But numerous studies find that children who live with a mother and her unmarried partner show significantly higher levels of problem behavior both at home and school—as well as lower overall academic performance than children who live with a married mother and father.[18]

Little Renaldo enjoys less security and routine in his home because his mother has had two new live-in boyfriends, one after the other, during his third-grade year. Renaldo is getting to be a bigger boy; his schoolwork is getting a little more difficult, and he really wants to excel. "They do real work in Mrs. Sanchez's class," he says. "No more coloring and having stories read to us like we're babies. We're third-graders now!" Indeed. And Renaldo takes it very seriously.

But he has a hard time leaving at home the emotional tumult of his home life: getting used to two new men in his life—and experiencing how these new relationships take more of his mother's time and attention. And he shows many signs of wondering where he now fits in a home that used to be about just him and Mom. If school is like an academic marathon, Renaldo's home situation this year is like giving him a pair of running shoes that weigh considerably more than those of his fellow students.

Delinquency levels and problems in school are highest among adolescents in cohabiting, stepfather families, when compared with married families and true single-parent families. Compared with their peers with married parents, teens in cohabiting homes had 122 percent greater odds of being expelled from school and delinquency. Delinquency rates are much lower for teens living with a truly single mother than with a cohabiting mother. And youths with cohabiting parents are 90 percent more likely to earn lower grades and have lower expectations of attending college.[19]

"The results . . . suggest that teenagers living with unmarried mothers do not seem to benefit from the presence of their mother's cohabiting partner," these researchers say. In fact, "These . . . findings reflect the importance of formal marital status" for a child's well-being.

It seems his mom's lifestyle choice is like giving Renaldo not only weighted shoes but also a backpack filled with rocks. A marriage license matters for children.

Other studies have rated the scores for various general but important well-being measures—and found that children who live with cohabiting parents are more similar to children living with single and remarried parents than to those who live with married parents.[20]

The respected Fragile Families research project, conducted at Princeton and Columbia Universities, teaches us that "children born to cohabiting parents have more aggressive, withdrawn and anxious/depressive behaviors at age three than children born to married parents." *Age three!* The negative impact is measurable early in a child's life.

And even if marriage follows a cohabiting birth, these scholars report, this did not translate into better child outcomes. This may point to how the early experience of cohabitation shapes a family relationship in unhealthy ways that persist even after a marriage finally takes place.[21] According to professor Linda Waite, children in cohabiting homes suffer significantly poorer overall mental health—from mild to more serious levels—than children who live with married parents.[22]

WEAK RELATIONSHIPS
HURT CHILDREN

Family formation experts consistently find that family stability makes a tremendous difference in how children fare in the home.[23] The more stable the home, the better children do. This means that a cohabiting, divorced, or single-parent home—by its very nature—might not be able to provide the benefits that a stable, first-time married home provides.

But a relatively stable cohabiting or single-parent home is more likely to provide better things for both the adults and children than one—like Renaldo's—where new partnerships are beginning and ending every few years. Children like stability. And this creates more bad news for cohabiting relationships.

Cohabiting families are less ideal for meeting children's development needs than married families, primarily because they are remarkably more unstable. This nearly guarantees these children will face at least one—if not more—family upheavals over a relatively short time.[24] Children born to cohabiting parents see the breakup of their homes at dramatically higher levels than those in married homes.[25]

Likelihood of Home Dissolution
by Child Age/Parent Relationship

Age of Child	Cohabiting Parents	Married Parents
1 year old	15%	4%
5 years old	50%	15%
10 years old	66%	29%

Compared to their peers with married parents, children with cohabiting parents are 292 percent more likely to see their parents break up.

And if their cohabiting parents do eventually marry, that risk of disruption drops—but is still 151 percent greater than for children born to married-only parents.[26] This remains true across racial and ethnic groups. A study of relationships in Norway—where cohabitation is much more common and accepted than marriage—found that children in cohabiting homes are nearly two and a half times more likely to see their parents break up than children with married parents. And this has remained consistent over several decades.[27]

"Nearly one in two cohabiting parents split up before a child's fifth birthday compared to one in twelve married parents," says the massive *State of the Nation Report* from the United Kingdom, and "three quarters of family breakdown affecting young children now involves unmarried parents."[28] Such upheaval harms children in many important measures of their development and well-being.[29]

Three-quarters of children who live with both unmarried parents will see them break up before they reach age sixteen. In contrast, only a third of children born to married parents will see their parents divorce.[30]

For at least a fourth of their childhood, those born into cohabiting homes are likely to live with only one parent. And when they grow up, the children of cohabiting parents will face a greater likelihood of divorce in their own marriages.[31]

Going through a pregnancy, then bringing an infant into the home, affects a couple's relationship. Typically this brings a couple closer together—even while their relationship goes through the significant transitions, struggles, and joys of parenthood.

But research into how babies affect cohabiting relationships reveals a different story. While conception tends to strengthen the link between the man and woman, the actual birth of the baby had no such effect.

"Children born in cohabiting unions do not influence family stability during cohabitation, but tend to have a destabilizing effect [even] when couples make the transition from cohabitation to marriage," the study concludes.[32] Conception and pregnancy—as a relatively short experience—was all that served as a positive influence upon cohabiting relationships, which tend to be short-term anyway. The drama, excitement, and joy of the arrival of the couple's child had no cohesive effect on their relationship.

WHAT MATTERS TO ADULTS
VS. WHAT MATTERS TO CHILDREN

The professed commitment of marriage benefits the man and woman, their well-being, and the longevity of their relationships. But children are most affected by the *durability* and *stability* of their parents' relationship.

Marriage clearly makes the relationship more stable and healthy, protecting against poverty and the serious problems it produces. Marriage protects against domestic violence and physical and sexual abuse of the child. It also reduces the levels of behavioral and academic problems that may plague the child.

Marriage accomplishes all this by creating a tighter relational and emotional connection between the child and her parents—as well as between the mom and dad. If we are concerned for the welfare of children, we should also be greatly concerned about the dramatic growth of cohabitation as a domestic life choice. Cohabitation does not lead to a happy, healthy life for our children—or ourselves. We must face the reality that a parent's decision to cohabit shows a lack of love, care, and responsibility toward the child.

Professor Susan Brown explains from a recent study:

Research has demonstrated that neither marriage nor residing with two biological parents is in itself a sufficient condition, as children in married stepfamilies . . . and two biological-parent cohabiting families fare worse, on average, than do their counterparts in simple two-biological-parent married families.[33]

Children are best set to thrive, grow, and live a happy life when their mom and dad give them the lifelong gift of committing themselves to one another in their marriage—as well as the effort and self-denial it takes to make that marriage grow. The key is not the number of parents in a home, or even the love they share and provide, but the nature of the relationship between them.

As we have seen in many measures, the ambiguity of cohabiting relationships makes them less beneficial than single-parent homes. Especially when contrasted with these less-defined cohabiting-parent households, marriage—with its stronger commitment and cohesion—makes a dramatic difference in *every* important measure of child well-being.[34]

QUESTIONS
for Couples

1. Even if you don't yet have children—and don't intend to have them in the near future—how do you think the factors that negatively impact children in cohabiting homes could help or hurt your own relationship with your partner?

2. Why might it be reasonable to think that things in your relationship that might be harmful for children might also be harmful to you?

3. How do you think factors about a couple's current cohabiting relationship could affect—for good or for bad—the kind of parents they may eventually become?

4. Why do you think domestic violence against children is higher in cohabiting homes?

5. What are some reasons why you'd explain that poverty is so much higher in cohabiting homes than in married homes?

RECOMMENDED RESOURCES

David Popenoe, "Cohabitation, Marriage and Child Wellbeing: A Cross National Perspective," National Marriage Project, Rutgers University, 2008. www.virginia.edu/marriageproject/pdfs/ NMP2008CohabitationReport.pdf

Susan Brown, "Marriage and Child Well-Being: Research and Policy Perspectives," *Journal of Marriage and Family* 72 (2010): 1059–77.

"Young Children's Behavior Problems in Married and Cohabiting Families," *Fragile Families Research Brief* (Bendheim-Thoman Center for Research on Child Well-being, Princeton University, June 2005).

Cynthia Osborne and Sara McLanahan, "Partnership Instability and Child Well-Being," *Journal of Marriage and Family* 69 (2007): 1065–83.

Wendy D. Manning and Daniel T. Lichter, "Parental Cohabitation and Children's Economic Well-Being," *Journal of Marriage and Family* 58 (1996): 998–1010.

Wendy D. Manning, "Children and the Stability of Cohabiting Couples," *Journal of Marriage and Family* 66 (2004): 674–89.

Wendy D. Manning and Kathleen A. Lamb, "Adolescent Well-Being in Cohabiting, Married and Single-Parent Families," *Journal of Marriage and Family* 65 (2003): 876–93.

Andrew J. Cherlin, *The Marriage-Go-Round: The State of Marriage and the Family in America Today* (New York: Alfred A. Knopf, 2009).

Larry Bumpass and Hsien-Hen Lu, "Trends in Cohabitation and Implications for Children's Family Context in the United States," *Population Studies* 54 (2000): 29–41.

Thomas DeLeire and Ariel Kalil, "How Do Cohabiting Couples with Children Spend Their Money?" *Journal of Marriage and Family* 67 (2005): 286–95.

NOTES

1. W. Bradford Wilcox and Elizabeth Marquardt, "When Marriage Disappears: The New Middle America," The State of Our Unions, 2010, an annual report on marriage in America from the National Marriage Project (Charlotte, VA, University of Virginia, December 2010), 75, 95; David Popenoe and Barbara Dafoe Whitehead, *Should We Live Together? What Young Adults Need to Know about Cohabitation before Marriage*, National Marriage Project, Rutgers University, 2002, 8.

2. Susan L. Brown, "Family Structure and Child Well-Being: The Significance of Parental Cohabitation," *Journal of Marriage and Family* 66 (2004): 351–67.

3. Sheila Kennedy and Larry Bumpass, "Cohabitation and Children's Living Arrangements: New Estimates from the United States," *Demographic Research* 19 (2008): 1663–92.

4. Brown, 2004, 351–67.

5. David Popenoe, "The Evolution of Marriage and the Problems of Stepfamilies: A Biosocial Perspective," in Alan Booth and Judy Dunn, eds., *Stepfamilies: Who Benefits? Who Does Not?* (Hillsdale, NJ: Lawrence Erlbaum Associates, 1994), 5, 19.

6. Brown, 2004, 354.

7. Larry Bumpass, James A. Sweet, and Andrew Cherlin, "The Role of Cohabitation in Declining Marriage Rates," *Journal of Marriage and Family* 53 (1991): 913–27.

8. Andrea J. Sedlak, et al., *Fourth National Incidence Study of Child Abuse and Neglect (NIS–4): Report to Congress, Executive Summary.* Washington, DC: US Department of Health and Human Services, Administration for Children and Families (2010).

9. Catherine Malkin and Michael Lamb, "Child Maltreatment: A Test of Sociobiological Theory," *Journal of Comparative Family Studies* 25 (1994): 121–33.

10. Michael Stiffman et al., "Household Composition and Risk of Fatal Child Maltreatment," *Pediatrics* 109 (2002): 615–21.

11. Leslie Margolin, "Child Abuse and Mother's Boyfriends: Why the Overrepresentation?" *Child Abuse and Neglect* 16 (1992): 541–51.

12. Popenoe and Whitehead, 2002, 8.

13. Michael Gordon and Susan J. Creighton, "Natal and Nonnatal Fathers as Sexual Abusers in the United Kingdom: A Comparative Analysis," *Journal of Marriage and Family* 50 (1988): 99.

14. Wendy D. Manning and Daniel T. Lichter, "Parental Cohabitation and Children's Economic Well-Being," *Journal of Marriage and Family* 58 (1996): 998–1010.

15. David Ellwood, *Poor Support: Poverty in the American Family* (New York: Basic Books, 1988), 46.

16. Quoted by James Q. Wilson, "Why We Don't Marry," *City Journal*, winter 2002. http://www.city-journal.org/html/12_1_why_we.html

17. Thomas DeLeire and Ariel Kalil, "How Do Cohabiting Couples with Children Spend Their Money?" *Journal of Marriage and Family* 67 (2005): 286–95.

18. Popenoe and Whitehead, 2002, 8.

19. Wendy D. Manning and Kathleen A. Lamb, "Adolescent Well-Being in Cohabiting, Married and Single-Parent Families," *Journal of Marriage and Family* 65 (2003): 876–93.

20. Donna Ruane Morrison and Amy Ritualo, "Routes Children's Economic Recovery after Divorce: Are Cohabitation and Remarriage Equivalent?" *American Sociological Review* 65 (2000): 560–80; Manning and Lichter, 1996, 1005, 1009; Manning and Lamb, 2003, 878–79.

21. "Young Children's Behavior Problems in Married and Cohabiting Families," *Fragile Families Research Brief* (Bendheim-Thoman Center for Research on Child Wellbeing, Princeton University, June 2005), 2–3.

22. Linda J. Waite and Maggie Gallagher, *The Case for Marriage: Why Married People Are Happier, Healthier, and Better Off Financially* (New York: Doubleday, 2000), 132.

23. Cynthia Osborne and Sara McLanahan, "Partnership Instability and Child Well-Being," *Journal of Marriage and Family* 69 (2007): 1065–83; Andrew J. Cherlin, *The Marriage-Go-Round: The State of Marriage and the Family in America Today* (New York: Alfred A. Knopf, 2009), 10–12.

24. Osborne and McLanahan, 2007, 1065, 1079.

25. Wendy D. Manning, Pamela J. Smock, and Debarun Majumdar, "The Relative Stability of Cohabiting and Marital Unions for Children," *Population Research and Policy Review* 23 (2004): 135–59.

26. Manning et al., 2004, 146, 151.

27. An-Magritt Jensen and Sten-Erick Clausen, *Children and Family Disruption in Norway: The Impact of Consensual Unions, Childhood* (Thousand Oaks, CA: Sage Publications, 2003), 65–81. Cited in David Popenoe's "Cohabitation, Marriage and Child Wellbeing: A Cross National Perspective," National Marriage Project, Rutgers University, 2008, 14.

28. *The State of the Nation Report: Fractured Families* (UK: Social Policy Justice Group, 2006), 9–13. Cited in Popenoe, 2008, 14.

29. Osborne and McLanahan, 2007.

30. Popenoe and Whitehead, 2002, 8; Larry Bumpass and Hsien-Hen Lu, "Trends in Cohabitation and Implications for Children's Family Contexts in the U.S.," *Population Studies* 54 (2000): 29–41.

31. James Q. Wilson, *The Marriage Problem: How Our Culture Has Weakened Families* (New York: HarperCollins, 2002), 6; Bumpass and Lu, 2000, 29–41.

32. Wendy D. Manning, "Children and the Stability of Cohabiting Couples," *Journal of Marriage and Family* 66 (2004): 674–89.

33. Susan Brown, "Marriage and Child Well-Being: Research and Policy Perspectives," *Journal of Marriage and Family* 72 (2010): 1059–77.

34. Brown, 2004, 364.

RATHER than a ball and chain

that weighs us down, marriage lifts our

physical and psychological health,

speeds our recoveries from illnesses,

and enhances our overall happiness.

6

MARRIAGE, HEALTH, AND HAPPINESS

I T IS ONE OF THE MOST fundamental and universally recognizable oaths of the wedding vow. The promise to love one another in sickness and in health—whether it's our own sickness or health or that of our beloved. This vow anticipates that things might not always go as we wish. Illness could come. And if it does, the couple is making a public declaration that in such a circumstance, no matter how trying or devastating, we will be there for our spouse—for the duration. This is a very comforting promise.

Everyone wants to enjoy good health. It's a profoundly important quality of life. People want to know how they can enhance their health—and with it, their happiness. Each week, we buy millions of copies of magazines and books so we can discover how.

But few people understand how much our most meaningful relationships contribute to—or distract from—our health and happiness. Researchers have been looking at the link between relationship status and well-being for more than 150 years. And the more sophisticated their examinations, the stronger their conclusions. What they find is that the nature of our relationship—whether we are married or just living together—makes a profound difference at nearly all levels for our overall health and happiness.

The relationship that brings us to vow our absolute commitment to another—in both sickness and health—forms a significant mechanism in not only keeping us from sickness but also in promoting greater health.

My wife and I have some good friends we have known for nearly twenty years. Mark and Florence are a bit younger than we are. We met them when we had our first child, who loved playing with their little beagle puppy. At the time they did not have any kids, and they enjoyed practicing being parents by occasionally watching Olivia for us.

Their family has since grown to a small gaggle of girls, just as ours has grown. They live in another city, a few miles away, so we don't see them as often as we would like. But we keep up with each other.

They have had significant news for us to keep up with, as they have both experienced some critical medical issues. For the past decade, Mark has suffered bouts of severe depression.

He has always been highly successful in his profession—kind of scary successful, able to hit home runs nearly every week without seeming to break a sweat. Naturally gifted, he knew how to use his abilities well.

But his struggles with depression—and trying to get his combination of meds just right—has knocked him down quite a few rungs, down to where most of us live. This has proved another struggle for him. He doesn't like being so heavily medicated just to function at normal.

Early in the process, Mark was tempted to go off his meds, which he did occasionally, to sometimes horrific effect. Each time it took him a while to stabilize, and that took a toll on his wife and children.

They are all very much in the struggle together. Florence has been a remarkable wife and friend, hanging in there with Mark as he navigated his ups and downs. He doubts he could have stayed in the game without her support, love, and occasional kick in the pants.

But just recently Florence, who is still relatively young and in excellent shape, experienced a massive stroke. This was a tsunami in their lives, every one of them. For a frightening long time, it looked like Flo might remain in a coma. And if she did come out of it, she might have very little ability to speak, walk, or use her hands. Horribly scary!

Since that early diagnosis, Flo has made a remarkable recovery. But she is still not scheduled to return home from the hospital any time soon. She's having to re-learn how to speak, walk, and use her arms.

I think of how hard this must be, not just for her but for Mark and the girls. They have had to watch as this amazingly strong and beautiful woman was pushed to the bottom of the hill called adult independence and must find a way to climb back somewhere near the top.

We all know of people who have faced tremendous physical or emotional sicknesses that call for great commitment by themselves and everyone around them. Marriage gives us the security of tying another person to us—and us to them. But marriage itself also serves as a general wall of protection from illness in ways that cohabitation does not.

MARRIAGE AS A BALL AND CHAIN?

Before we start to examine what the research shows us, let's consider something. What does the phrase "ball and chain" mean to you? What type of relationship is it usually attached to? Right—being married. Does that phrase give you a positive or negative sense of the relationship? Keep this image in mind, and we will see how accurate this "ball and chain" perception of marriage actually is.

Let's start by looking at how cohabiting and marriage relationships affect our physical health and wellness.

HEALTH AND LONGEVITY

Overall, men and women who are married live longer and are less likely to have to visit their doctor or be referred for hospital care. Science finds that being married tends to motivate people to increase healthy behaviors, habits, and attitudes.

As a result, married people live longer. The "relationship between marriage and death rates has now reached the status of a truism," wrote University of Chicago sociologist Linda Waite, "having been observed across numerous societies and among various social and demographic groups." In an absolutely overwhelming mountain of evidence, she says, "we find a significant and sizable mortality disadvantage for both men and women who are not married compared to the married."[1] ("Mortality disadvantage" is sociologist-speak for dying sooner.)

The sheer weight of research on this point motivated Professor Waite to write her book *The Case for Marriage*. In it she updates her early research, stating, "The evidence from four decades of research is surprisingly clear: a good marriage is both men's and women's best bet for living a long and healthy life."[2]

Dr. Robert Coombs of UCLA reviewed more than 130 studies published over the past century on how marriage affects well-being. He found "an intimate link between marital status and personal well-being."[3]

> Virtually every study of mortality and marital status shows the unmarried of both sexes have higher death rates, whether by accident, disease, or self-inflicted wounds, and this is found in every country that maintains accurate health statistics.[4]

If marriage is a ball and chain, it appears to keep the threat of sickness and death tied down.

IF marriage is a ball and chain,

it appears to keep the threat of

sickness and death tied down.

Two British economists reviewed a host of studies on how marital status influences men's and women's overall health. A ten-year examination of British homes found that married people benefit from dramatically stronger levels of health and longevity. These scholars found that the health benefits married people enjoy was "enough to offset the risk of smoking for men, and enough to offset approximately half the risk for women."[5] How is that for dramatic?

Earlier studies by Yale University also showed that the health premium of marriage is powerful enough to cancel out such dramatic health threats as smoking.[6] One scholar joked that a married man considering divorce or taking up smoking had quite a dilemma.

Another remarkable conclusion—made in two different studies by economists—found that "marriage has a more important effect on longevity than income."[7] This is significant, considering how people with higher income can enjoy better levels of health care, relaxation, and healthy foods. A review of twenty-seven long-term and sixty-six "snapshot" studies confirmed that:

- Being married is associated with elevated levels of health and well-being.
- Marriage also increases one's likelihood of remaining healthy in the years and decades to come.[8]

This link was even stronger if the marriage was strong.

The protective influence of marriage applies not only to more minor illnesses like colds, flu, and migraine headaches but also to serious health issues like cancer, heart disease, and heart attacks—as well as the need for any kind of surgery.[9] Research published in the *Journal of the American Medical Association* pointed out that married cancer patients had quicker and more successful battles against cancer than their unmarried peers and that the health benefit from being married was equal to being in an age category ten years younger.[10]

A few studies show the health benefit is slightly stronger for men, but *healthy* marital relationships affect women more positively than men.

And while marriage relationships are shown to last longer than cohabiting relationships, the health benefits of marriage last longer as well.

Investigations of men and women in their retirement years found that "marriage is associated with better health across all major domains of health, and across all types of conditions within the domains of health." And these health benefits are "robust" across diverse socioeconomic, ethnic, and racial groups.[11]

Because social pressure to marry has lessened over the past few decades, a recent study investigated whether the mortality gap between the married and the unmarried might be shrinking. But it found that marrieds continue to maintain a constant advantage over the unmarrieds in nearly all health measures.[12]

So the reason for marriage's effect in people's health is not just that people view marriage as being more positive. Even in these days when marriage rates have declined, marriage continues to have just as strong a positive influence on people's well-being.

WHY THE MARRIAGE HEALTH PREMIUM?

Why does marriage produce these increased health benefits?

This is a big question in the research community. Some used to assume that healthier people were more likely to receive marriage proposals. This theory, called the "selection effect," has some common sense behind it. Aren't we all more likely to choose a husband or wife who is healthy and vibrant?

A competing view, the "protection/support" theory, asserts that marrieds are healthier because something about marriage itself increases the likelihood we will take better care of ourselves.

Which theory is correct?

This is where much discussion and debate exists among scholars. The question is not *whether* marriage is healthier than cohabitation but *why?* In the past ten to fifteen years, a respectable amount of evidence has landed more support on the side of marriage actually increasing our healthy behaviors and attitudes—as well as putting someone in our lives who is likely to encourage us in healthy ways.

"Social control" is a term sociologists use to refer to one person directing another's behavior. All people need this. In our early years, it is called parenting. But in our adult years, we still need it. And in our everyday adult domestic relationships, people call it "nagging."

By whatever name, it does keep us healthier. It involves advice like "Eat your vegetables," "Get a good night's sleep," "Don't drive so fast," "Wear your scarf and earmuffs!" and "How many donuts have you eaten today?" These words from a spouse may not always be welcomed, but they help us stay more healthy.

Professor Debra Umberson at the University of Texas, Austin, has done some of the most sophisticated work on this question—looking at the intersection of social control and marital status. She finds that having someone paying attention to what we do and don't do—and encouraging us to do the right thing—is good for us.

Umberson also discovered that women "nag" men more than men "nag" women. Are you surprised? And *wives* are much more likely to do this successfully than live-in girlfriends or even mothers. "Marriage may be beneficial to health," Umberson says, "because many spouses monitor and attempt to control their spouse's health behavior" while nonmarrieds don't do this as much.[13]

My friend Mark no doubt benefited because Florence kept after him to keep trying different combinations of antidepressants and asking his doctors to give him the guidance he needed to get to a healthy, stable place. She no doubt nagged him for his own well-being—but also for her own. She wanted a husband for herself and a daddy for their girls who was more stable emotionally.

While at the time it may not seem like a gift, having someone push us in healthy but uncomfortable directions is really a blessing.

Conversely, research looking specifically at cohabitors found that "there was no additional survival advantage for persons who lived with someone other than a spouse. . . . The critical factor for survival was the presence of a spouse."[14] Instead, cohabitors were more likely to resemble singles in their health and life span.

Now let's look at the levels of contentment and mental health that married people actually enjoy in their longer lives. If the "ball and chain" image of marriage is true, what is the advantage of living a long life if it's not happy?

HAPPINESS AND MENTAL HEALTH

As with physical health and longevity, a great deal of research has been done on how marital and relational status affects overall happiness and general mental health. And the findings are just as conclusive.

Crazy about You?

Reaching back as early as 1936, Benjamin Malzberg, the senior statistician for the New York State Department of Mental Hygiene, found that first-time admissions for psychiatric services were more than five times higher for the unmarried compared to their married peers. "The evidence seems clear," he said, "that the married population had, in general, much lower rates of mental disease than any of the other marital groups."[15]

More recent studies show the same thing. And these newer studies have the benefit of comparing married couples with their cohabiting peers. Professor Susan Brown, examining this connection closely, explains that "marital status is a key determinant of psychological well-being."[16] Levels of depression for cohabitors average about 2.8 points higher than for marrieds, even after controlling for important socioeconomic factors between the two groups. Women, nonwhites, and the young report the highest levels of depression among cohabitors.

Professor Brown discovered no support for the selection effect. Instead, "cohabitors' higher levels of depression are a function of their greater relationship instability relative to marrieds" as well as a "function of cohabitors' poorer relationship quality."[17]

Surprisingly, those cohabiting longer are worse off in terms of relational quality and lacking a sense of commitment than those who cohabit for shorter periods. This suggests that the experience of cohabiting tends to grow weaker and worse over time, rather than better and stronger.

Other scholars support Brown's findings of relational weakness. "Compared with married respondents and adjusted for duration and age differences, cohabitors are almost twice as likely to report that they have thought their relationship was in trouble in the past year . . . and in three of every four cohabiting relationships, at least one partner reports having thought the relationship was in trouble."[18] Women are more likely to have such feelings than their live-in boyfriends.

A major study of psychological well-being in America published in the 1990s found that rates of severe depression were lowest among those who were married only once (1.5 percent) and highest among the cohabiting (5.1 percent). The only group showing more depression than the cohabitors were those *twice* divorced (5.8 percent).[19] And the likelihood of suffering from *any* psychiatric disorder, according to this study, was more than twice as high for cohabiting individuals than their married peers.

"One of the most consistent findings in psychiatric epidemiology," according to research conducted at Yale and UCLA, "is that married persons enjoy better health than the unmarried." These scientists find the "association between marital status and mental illness is robust and generalizable" among major racial groups—and the mental health benefits of marriage were not seen in cohabiting couples.[20]

Happily Ever After?

A study of marital status and happiness in seventeen diverse industrialized nations (and controlling for variables such as education, income, poverty, and general health) found that being married was 3.4 times more closely associated with reports of general happiness and contentedness than cohabitation. This was true for men and women equally.[21] In his broad literature survey, Dr. Robert Coombs of UCLA found that "no part of the unmarried population . . . describes itself as being so happy and contented with life as the married."[22]

And economists found that being married increases overall happiness much like the boost one gets from having a substantially higher paycheck. One scholar likens it to the effect of a 2.5 times payroll increase. Another equates it to a specific dollar amount: an extra $100,000 dollars a year.

But cohabitation, according to both studies, did not create similar benefits.[23] *How remarkable is that?* One scholar reports this difference is because "cohabitation is significantly associated with greater levels of relational unfairness, relative unhappiness, and less frequent partner interaction," as well as higher levels of sexual infidelity.[24]

Additional work linked the differing levels of happiness to the rates of conflict between married couples and cohabitors. The two "differ in the frequency of conflict with [even] long-term cohabitors reporting the greatest frequency of conflict and long-term married individuals reporting the least."[25] In a similar vein, another study found that long-term cohabiting couples ranked "significantly lower" than married couples in regard to general happiness and feelings of relational fairness.[26]

But when couples move into more committed relationships such as marriage—where the markers of commitment are clear and distinct—they see noticeable improvements. "With respect to well-being, some [relational] commitment appears to be good, and more commitment appears to be better."[27]

Perhaps this information on how and why marriage improves health and happiness helps explain the findings of a recent survey by the Pew Research Center. Comparing various family forms in the United States, this large investigation found that "married people are more satisfied with their family lives than are unmarried people"—including the cohabiting.[28]

MARRIAGE IS MEDICAL

My friends Mark and Flo each battled a serious threat to their health. But Mark's psychiatrist and Florence's physicians and physical therapists would tell you their success in overcoming their ailments has come in large part because they have each invested so heavily in the other's life—and in their health struggles.

This is the promise they made to each other—to love and cherish in health, when everything is fine. But also to love and cherish in sickness—when things are tough. Neither Mark nor Flo had any idea when they exchanged those vows—nor did their parents, family, and friends who witnessed their wedding—how severely this part of their vow would be tested and relied upon.

It is a wonderful gift that we give to another . . . and in return, we give also to ourselves. The marriage vow does make a difference, as the wealth of research presented in this chapter shows.

Rather than a ball and chain that weighs us down, marriage—so much more than cohabitation—consistently lifts our physical and psychological health, keeps us away from doctors, speeds our recoveries from illness, and boosts our contentment.

Something that does all of these—so effectively and consistently—deserves our interest and involvement. The commitment that marriage asks of us helps us learn to care for others—and allows us to receive their care.

Marriage, and not cohabitation, is a gift that brings an abundance of health and happiness.

QUESTIONS
for Couples

1. Do you find it surprising that a marriage license has such a strong effect on a husband's and wife's health, while simply cohabiting does not?

2. What does it say to you that studies find that simply being married is like being ten years younger or having an extra $100,000 dollars a year? Or that the health benefits of marriage are strong enough to offset the health risks of smoking?

3. Why do you think the agreed-upon commitment of marriage makes such a significant difference in a couple's health?

4. How do you think the "social control/nagging" factor found by Professor Umberson works to make a couple safer and healthier? Do you agree with how this might work? Why or why not?

5. Given what you have learned, what would you tell friends who were considering cohabiting? Is that advice good enough for yourself?

RECOMMENDED RESOURCES

Linda J. Waite and Maggie Gallagher, *The Case for Marriage: Why Married People Are Happier, Healthier, and Better Off Financially* (New York: Doubleday, 2000).

Glenn T. Stanton, *Why Marriage Matters: Reasons to Believe in Marriage in Postmodern Society* (Colorado Springs: NavPress, 1997).

Steven Stack and J. Ross Eshleman, "Marital Status and Happiness: A 17-Nation Study," *Journal of Marriage and Family* 60 (1998): 527–36.

Robert Coombs, "Marital Status and Personal Well-Being: A Literature Review," *Family Relations* 40 (1991): 97–102.

Hui Liu, "Till Death Do Us Part: Marital Status and U.S. Mortality Trends, 1986-2000," *Journal of Marriage and Family* 71 (2009): 1158–73.

Laura Stafford, Susan L. Kline, and Caroline T. Rankin, "Married Individuals, Cohabitors and Cohabitors Who Marry: A Longitudinal Study of Relational and Individual Well-Being," *Journal of Social and Personal Relationships* 21 (2004): 231–48.

Susan L. Brown, "The Effects of Union Type on Psychological Well-Being: Depression among Cohabitors versus Marrieds," *Journal of Health and Social Behaviors* 41 (2000): 241–55.

NOTES

1. Lee A. Lillard and Linda J. Waite, "Till Death Do Us Part: Marital Disruption and Mortality," *American Journal of Sociology* 100 (1995): 1131–56.

2. Linda J. Waite and Maggie Gallagher, *The Case for Marriage: Why Married People Are Happier, Healthier, and Better Off Financially* (New York: Doubleday, 2000), 64.

3. Robert Coombs, "Marital Status and Personal Well-Being: A Literature Review," *Family Relations* 40 (1991): 97–102.

4. Coombs, 1991, 98.

5. Chris M. Wilson and Andrew J. Oswald, "How Does Marriage Affect Physical and Psychological Health? A Survey of the Longitudinal Evidence," *Institute for the Study of Labor Study Paper* 1619 (Bonn, Germany: Institute for the Study of Labor, May 2005), 16.

6. Harold J. Morowitz, "Hiding in the Hammond Report," *Hospital Practice* (August 1975): 39.

7. Jonathan Gardner and Andrew Oswald, "How Is Mortality Affected by Money, Marriage and Stress?" *Journal of Health Economics* 23 (2004): 1181–207.

8. Christine M. Proulx, Heather Helms, and Cheryl Buehler, "Marital Quality and Personal Well-Being: A Meta-Analysis," *Journal of Marriage and Family* 69 (2007): 576–93.

9. Janice K. Kiecolt-Glaser and Tamara L. Newton, "Marriage and Health: His and Hers," *Psychological Bulletin* 127 (2001): 472–503.

10. James S. Goodwin, William C. Hunt, Charles R. Key, and Jonathan M. Samet, "The Effect of Marital Status on Stage, Treatment and Survival of Cancer Patients," *Journal of the American Medical Association* 258 (1987): 3125–30.

11. Amy Mehraban Pienta et al., "Health Consequences of Marriage for the Retirement Years," *Journal of Family Issues* 21 (2000): 559–86.

12. Hui Liu, "Till Death Do Us Part: Marital Status and U.S. Mortality Trends, 1986–2000," *Journal of Marriage and Family* 71 (2009): 1158–73.

13. Debra Umberson, "Gender, Marital Status and the Social Control of Health Behavior," *Social Science Medicine* 34 (1992): 907–17; Debra Umberson et al., "The Effect of Social Relationships on Psychological Well-Being: Are Men and Women Really So Different?" *American Sociological Review* 61 (1996): 837–57.

14. Maradee A. Davis et al., "Living Arrangements and Survival among Middle-Aged and Older Adults in the NHANES I Epidemiologic Follow-up Study," *American Journal of Public Health* 82 (1992): 401–6.

15. Benjamin Malzberg, "Marital Status in Relation to the Prevalence of Mental Disease," *Psychiatric Quarterly* 10 (1936): 245–56.

16. Susan L. Brown, "The Effects of Union Type on Psychological Well-Being: Depression among Cohabitors versus Marrieds," *Journal of Health and Social Behaviors* 41 (2000): 241–55.

17. Brown, 2000, 253.

18. Larry L. Bumpass, James A. Sweet, and Andrew Cherlin, "The Role of Cohabitation in Declining Rates of Marriage," *Journal of Marriage and Family* 53 (1991): 913–27.

19. Lee Robins and Darrel Regier, *Psychiatric Disorders in America: The Epidemiologic Catchment Area Study* (New York: Free Press, 1991), 64, 334.

20. David R. Williams et al., "Marital Status and Psychiatric Disorders among Black and Whites," *Journal of Health and Social Behavior* 33 (1992): 140–57.

21. Steven Stack and J. Ross Eshleman, "Marital Status and Happiness: A 17-Nation Study," *Journal of Marriage and Family* 60 (1998): 527–36.

22. Coombs, 1991, 100.

23. Wilson and Oswald, May 2005, 1; Bruce Wydick, "Grandma Was Right: Why Cohabitation Undermines Relational Satisfaction, but Is Increasing Anyway," *Kyklos* 60 (2007): 617–45.

24. Wydick, 2007, 621.

25. Laura Stafford, Susan L. Kline, and Caroline T. Rankin, "Married Individuals, Cohabitors and Cohabitors Who Marry: A Longitudinal Study of Relational and Individual Well-Being," *Journal of Social and Personal Relationships* 21 (2004): 231–48.

26. Kevin B. Skinner et al., "Cohabitation, Marriage and Remarriage: A Comparison of Relationship Quality Over Time," *Journal of Family Issues* 23 (2002): 74–90.

27. Claire M. Kamp-Dush and Paul R. Amato, "Consequences of Relationship Status and Quality for Subjective Well-Being," *Journal of Social and Personal Relationships* 22 (2005): 607–27.

28. "The Decline of Marriage and Rise of New Families," *Pew Research Center*, November 2010, 18.

WOMEN are more likely
to see their cohabiting relationships as
a conveyor belt eventually leading to
marriage. Guys are more likely to see
their cohabiting relationships as
the opportunity to see each other
more often, have fun together,
make sure he feels taken care of,
and gain access to more regular sex.

7

COHABITATION:
THE RELATIONSHIP
ON THE GUY'S TERMS?

G UYS AND GALS NEED to know who the cohabiting relationship favors and how. Because it certainly favors one over the other—
significantly so. And that leaves the other one holding the short end of
the stick—not really good in such an intimate relationship. In the following pages we will explore the ups and downs of this so that both guys
and gals can be better informed about their standing in the cohabitation
relationship.

HOW MODERN
FEMINISM FAILED WOMEN

Modern feminism developed in the 1960s as a way to strengthen the
standing and opportunities of women in society, a highly praiseworthy
goal. But in developing their philosophy and strategy for lifting the status
of women, feminism got way off the rails by adopting some very anti-
woman positions.

Let's look at three in particular, with the third touching directly on
our topic in this book.

Abortion

Abortion as a "sacrament" was the first of these. While that sounds shocking, this is exactly how key feminist leaders proclaimed it.[1]

To this point of view, pregnancy—a powerful, profound, and uniquely feminine quality—was seen not as a virtue but rather as a weakness to overcome: How could women keep up if they were constantly being dragged down by bearing children? These nice folks completely overlooked how a woman's ability to give the world the next generation of humanity might not be a weakness but rather a tremendous power.

Women who came of age since the 1960s and '70s—many of them raised by these very feminists—have taken a more honest and higher view of their fertility. As this happens, support for abortion among young women has been slipping in recent years.[2]

Women increasingly see from their own experience—and by the experiences of their friends and even their mothers—that abortion has not liberated women. "For those of us in our twenties," says cultural analyst Dawn McBane, "the issue of abortion hits very close to home. We are the generation who lost friends and siblings, which is one reason why I believe our generation will continue to be the most pro-life generation in history."

They have seen in painfully dramatically ways that abortion might remove a developing baby from your womb, but does not remove the growing child from your heart. Pregnancy, women are realizing, is far more than a mere physiological function that we can simply stop one day because we will it.

The woman with child—even in the earliest days—finds that something is happening not just in her uterus but also throughout her entire body—even her heart and soul. This is why the news of a pregnancy is never met with indifference but usually with joy, excitement, and even nervousness. Sometimes it is met with great fear. But the woman's response is never lukewarm.

As Melanie, a young Asian journalist working in China, told me about her abortion, "Every part of my body and heart were preparing to help my baby grow, even in those early days. That child is gone from under my heart, but it is still very much in my heart."

Sexual Expressiveness

Sexual expressiveness was the second development blessed by the feminists. Back in the day, we were told it was fine for a man to show up on his wedding night with his virginity long gone. But we had names for gals who could not honestly wear white on their big day. *A clear double standard, right?*

The feminist solution was not to have men behave more virtuously but to encourage women to act more like men sexually. Women would no longer be sexual victims if they also became sexually aggressive. This was supposed to be empowerment.

But guess what? It ended up hurting women as they played into the male sexual script. In the past decade, a number of very strong—and for some, unexpected—books have appeared on how this leveling of the sexual playing field has played itself out.

The first, *Unprotected*, by UCLA campus psychiatrist Miriam Grossman, M.D., explains how she found herself increasingly angry and disgusted by how the campus hookup culture was ravaging the bodies, hearts, and psyches of students at her school.

To those who believe that men and women are essentially the same, save for some obvious plumbing differences, her book seems to hold a dramatic bias against male students. Why? She explains that her patients —the students who regularly made their way through her office for physical and emotional help from their frequent and casual sexual exchanges— were mostly women: "My argument is simple," Dr. Grossman writes. "If someone's my patient, I'm responsible for her—all of her."[3]

Why *her*? It is as if she automatically uses that pronoun to describe patients, without a thought about *him*. This is not because she doesn't care about the harm that easy sexuality does to boys but rather because she is less likely to see them coming into her office. Her waiting room is mostly filled with girls.

Both men and women are harmed by sexuality set free from the protective harbor of the commitment, safety, and dignity that marriage provides. But it is much more damaging to young women—on so many levels

—than it is to young men. This is because sex is a much different experience to a woman. Think about why that might be.

Another book on the harm caused by today's sexual attitudes is *Unhooked*, by Pulitzer Prize–winning *Washington Post* journalist Laura Sessions Stepp. She draws from her extensive research and interviews with college-age men and women at leading universities and how they are experiencing the "hookup culture" in which both young men and women are expected to engage in sexual relationships that are quick, clean, and impersonal.

But Stepp discovered what the author of *Unprotected* also found. "The girls I observed," Stepp says, "almost always ended up disappointed" by these emotionless, commitment-free sexual exchanges. And, "Although they don't admit it readily, young men are as dissatisfied with hooking up as young women."[4]

But the girls carry the emptiness of it in deeper ways. Stepp introduces her readers to Alicia, a junior at Duke, who explained with sad honesty:

> From the time I lost my virginity until now, it's only been the guy getting pleasure. . . . More guys have had sex with me than I have sex with them. . . .[5]

Doesn't that break your heart for Alicia? Is this the kind of sister-empowerment the 1960s feminists envisioned? Why does Alicia subject herself to this? Because she thinks she's supposed to. The feminists thought they were so smart, but they miserably failed to appreciate the complexity of both the nature of sexuality as well as the depths of the feminine heart.

Another student Stepp introduces us to spoke of having become so bored with sex that she actually read a magazine while guys had their way with her. A brilliant woman with status, she was gaining a world-class education—but how different was she from a prostitute? At least prostitutes believe their sexuality has a market value. She didn't want to be there, but she regularly submitted herself to it. Why? When was the last time you read something so tragic about young adult relationships, but this is increasingly common for young women today.

And a young man, a senior at George Washington University, told Stepp what kind of effect this changing sexual economy was having on him and his male peers: "Because girls are more assertive (sexually), it's easy for us to be [jerks]."[6] God help us.

Professor Donna Freitas wrote the third of these books, *Sex & the Soul*. She teaches religion at Hofstra University and has studied college students across the country on their experiences and views on sexuality. She told me that more and more, as young women become sexually aggressive and experienced, they are not enjoying or being fulfilled by the experience. "They slowly learn to shut themselves down emotionally, so much so that they don't even seem to feel anymore. They tell me time after time that they feel they can't afford to."[7]

> Amy expresses a consuming frustration when it comes to sex and romance, and begins to seem less like a princess and more like the average college woman I met—vulnerable, burned by at least one guy and who, behind closed doors, admits to regret, shame and dismay. . . . Amy also shares an inability to find her heart's desire: a real boyfriend, one who loved and respected her and who would admit to their relationship in public by doing something as simple as asking her on a date or holding her hand while walking across campus.[8]

Like Alicia, Amy was deeply scarred by what she wrote about in her journal one day. Of her last sexual encounter, she lamented that "We were not connecting."

So many of these bright women, like Amy, say that if they could have a relationship on their terms, it would be one of traditional dates, holding hands, laughter, lightness, and genuine closeness.

The feminist advice of diving into the deep end of the sexual revolution has proved a tragic cruelty to women. And isn't this just what the misogynist publishers of glossy "men's magazines" had in mind for their own selfish pleasure: getting girls to become more sexually open? It was as if the modern feminist leaders—and the millions of young women they led —became captive puppets tied to the manipulating strings of very bad men.

Let's Live Together

Cohabitation was the third development of the feminist brain trust. Many factors led to its quick rise in the 1960s and '70s. Among the earliest was the feminist thinking that marriage oppressed women because when the matrimony door slammed shut, it trapped millions of women in lifelong relationships of drudgery: cleaning house, cooking meals, washing dishes, chasing after hoards of children, providing sex to their husbands on demand, and saying good-bye to nearly all of their important goals and dreams. That was the picture they cast.

Cohabitation, they believed, could fix all this. It was finally the relationship where the woman came as an equal player. The couple would bring both their incomes into their home piggy bank and share them equally. Rising above the oppression of the old domestic gender-order, the man and woman would equally split the drudgery of household chores. And because the woman could leave the no-strings-attached relationship at any time, the man would be more likely to treat her the way she wanted to be treated. If not, she could be gone tomorrow to a better man. Doesn't that make sense?

As with abortion and sexual expressiveness, we have had decades to see how these ideas about cohabitation actually worked out. As we have seen through these pages, cohabitation has nothing really good to offer either men or women. But there is a great deal of research showing that cohabitation has failed in nearly every way to live up to feminists' high ideals.

THERE is a great deal of

research showing that cohabitation

has failed in nearly every way

to live up to feminists' high ideals.

The information we examine in this chapter shows that, generally, marriage establishes the relationship on the woman's terms, while cohabitation establishes the relationship on the man's terms. This is important for women to know for themselves, for their girlfriends, and also for their daughters. Let's look at why scientists are confirming what our grandmas took as common sense all along. Let's start with the biggest topic in relationships.

COMMITMENTS: PUBLIC PROMISES MATTER

Everyone agrees that cohabiting relationships are less committed than marital relationships. Couples are freer to end the relationship and move to greener pastures. But what few appreciate is that the level of commitment in cohabiting relationships differs for men and women. Consider this:

Gather a group of one hundred cohabiting couples from various parts of the country and socioeconomic backgrounds. Tell these couples you want to talk to them and learn about the future of their relationship— where they are going. You divide the group, taking all the women to one interview room and all the men to another.

Ask each group to describe their relational goals and expectations. Where would they like to be in a year or so? The interviewers then take all the men's answers and the women's answers, match them by couples, then compare their answers. How similar do you think the men's and the women's intentions would be for their relational futures?

Researchers have done exactly this. Which of these three sets of intentions do you think they found?

1. Cohabiting men and women—at largely the same levels—both hoped to move their relationship to marriage as soon as possible.
2. Cohabiting men and women felt they were just having fun with their relationship and didn't want to rush things.
3. Cohabiting men and women had very different views of where they thought their relationship was going.

Which did you pick? If you are a woman, it is very important for your own sense of equality to know that number three was what these researchers found. This remained true across racial, ethnic, and socio-economic groups. Women are consistently more likely to see their cohabiting relationships as a conveyor belt eventually leading to marriage. And for most women, better sooner than later.

Guys were more likely to see their cohabiting relationships as the opportunity to see each other more often, have fun together, feel taken care of by their gal, and gain access to more regular sex. For men, marriage wasn't off the table, but it could come later. And "later" usually continues to get even later. The guys were having fun today—getting largely what they want—so why rush things?

In one major study, female cohabitors were more than three times more likely than their boyfriends to speak of "love" as the foundation of their relationship. Guys were four times more likely to explain that sex was an important objective in their cohabiting relationship. As one man told these researchers, "You moved in for it, [so] just roll over and get it." Ladies, I can hear your hearts swoon with that sentiment!

Another man said, "I think in a lot of people's heads, we are actually [living together] to have easier access to sex and to be with one another as much as we want."[9]

Even among cohabitors who both value marriage, recent research finds it is quite common for the men to be less dedicated to the relationship than their girlfriends—even if they said they eventually plan to marry.

In these relationships, researchers say, "Women may be at a disadvantage in terms of relational power because they are the ones that are more committed." They warn further:

Particularly if they are unaware of the difference in commitment, women may wind up making more sacrifices for their relationships than their partners, and these unrequited sacrifices could be detrimental if the relationship ends.[10]

Men and women value their relationships differently. And men and women also tend to have more than just differing views on where the relationship is headed and how long it will take to get there. They also tend to have an imbalance of strength in the union, with the man typically having "more power to determine whether the relationship ends in marriage."[11] The woman is more likely to be left to hope.

These professional research findings connect tightly with observations made by a journalist who interviewed many cohabiting couples for the book she wrote to guide people through the thickets of cohabiting relationships. In *A Little Bit Married*, Hannah Seligson spends considerable time helping her readers learn how they might move the relationship from the boyfriend/girlfriend stage to the husband/wife stage. But as with the UCLA campus psychiatrist in *Unprotected*, she spends not one word speaking to guys on how to get the girl serious about marriage. Does she not care about helping guys get that special gal to make the marital plunge? Is she sexist, interested only in helping the girls? You and I know better, don't we?

It is not through shortsightedness or sexism that her chapter titled "Are We There Yet?" is subtitled "The Female Proposal." And for Hannah Seligson, the female proposal is not for the girl to step up and pop the question herself. Her female proposal is an ultimatum: Set a deadline: girl, if a ring is not delivered by a specific date, show your guy what these boots are made for.

Seligson introduces us to Dari, a headstrong twenty-eight-year-old woman who has lost count of how many "where is this relationship going?" conversations she has had with her live-in boyfriend. Dari came to realize that "the ultimatum is a power tool."

But I like what Seligson calls the "2.0 iteration of the ultimatum" as used by Ashley when she was a midtwenties single. It puts *her* in the driver's seat from the start of the relationship: "I told my boyfriend . . . that I'd gotten into graduate school, and I wanted him to move in with me, but I wanted us to be married before we did."[12] Guess what, ladies? He went for it. And they've now been married for more than ten years.

Who do you think is wearing the capri pants in these two relationships: Dari with the 1.0 ultimatum of "I'm tired of being your live-in girlfriend, dude!" or Ashley with her 2.0 upgrade of "I'm setting the terms here, Chuck, and the choice is yours. Take me as your wife or don't take me at all!"? Ashley knew her own worth, and she made sure she got the full market value. Do you think she has any regrets? She knew what she wanted, she went after it on her terms, and she got it. And she did it by refusing the feminist script. Imagine!

IMPACT ON THE MARRIAGE

But Dari might also get what she wants: a ring on her finger by a certain date and the transformation of her live-in boyfriend to a husband. She might . . . but the research tells us she will likely pay a heavier price in her marriage that Ashley won't be strapped with.

Not only are cohabiting men overwhelmingly less interested in moving the relationship to marriage as quickly as their girlfriends, but they also become different kinds of husbands if they do marry. This is a fact that women have a right to know.

COHABITING men are
less interested in marriage,
and if they do marry,
they become different kinds of husbands.

A professional journal article—titled "Maybe I Do"—by three leading cohabitation scholars from the University of Denver explains a strong finding consistent with other investigations: "Men who premaritally cohabited with their wives, were on average, a good deal less dedicated to their wives *even once they are married!*" (emphasis in original).

The sex difference concerning after-marriage commitment was stark: "It is quite notable that this difference was not observed at all in females."[13] Get that. "Not *at all* in females." And compared with their noncohabiting married peers, males who cohabited before marriage had "significantly higher levels" of negative interactions with their wives, as well as increased incidences of domestic violence against them.

Additional research by this team found that cohabitors who eventually married displayed a higher degree of unhealthy problem-solving skills and lower degrees of spousal support. Both can seriously deplete the health of the marriage and tend to develop increased feelings of bitterness and resentment.[14]

Cohabiting couples are prone to drag bad habits into their marriage. Walter, who lived with Wilma for eighteen months, learned how to be a particular kind of partner because of the nature of his relationship with Wilma—a relationship with a lack of clarity and commitment. And when Walter did finally become her husband, the marriage made a difference—as marriage does.

But those eighteen months of cohabitation still had an impact. Walter learned certain behaviors because of the attitudes he developed about the relationship. And Walter carried these behaviors and attitudes from their cohabiting phase into their marriage. And that affects his behavior as a husband. And Wilma has to live with the consequences.

This means that if a woman wants a way to significantly increase the likelihood of getting a husband who:

1. is less committed than she is to the marriage
2. is less committed to her and to marriage than noncohabiting husbands
3. displays unhealthy problem-solving skills
4. is less likely to be emotionally and practically supportive
5. is more generally relationally negative and
6. displays violent behavior toward her . . .

. . . then the science tells us that living with a future husband before marriage is one of the most efficient ways to get each of these. And all this by just living with him first!

A COHABITATIONAL VORTEX?

This startling result brings up an important aspect of cohabitation that scholars are just now discovering. Some women might read this research and comfort themselves by saying, "If I discover all this about my guy while we are living together, isn't it better to learn it before I make the big leap into marriage?"

Some of the leading research indicates that the process of cohabiting itself can create these negative experiences in both men and women, but more likely for the guy.[15] And we are finding that cohabiting couples can get caught in a vortex that scholars call "relational inertia."

This phenomenon can tend to trap the couple in an unhealthy sort of gravitational pull—emotionally, financially, physically, and supportively—that keeps them from being able to break off a relationship they agree is less than what they want and need.[16] And many of these unhealthy relationships end up in marriage—with the couple sliding into, rather than deciding to enter, marriage—just as many of them simply slid into their original cohabiting relationship.

Professor Scott Stanley says that just as natural physics dictates that it's harder to stop a rolling ten-ton truck than a VW bug, relational physics states that "it simply must be harder to end the average cohabiting relationship than it is to end a dating relationship." Explaining how this affects marriage, Stanley says:

> Cohabitation puts the average couple on a trajectory toward marriage and it may be difficult to exit that trajectory, even if the relationship doesn't have what it takes to make a marriage happy or lasting. The potential [negative] implications of this inertia are great.[17]

This can set women up for unexpected, deep disappointment, says Galena Kline Rhoades, because women are more likely to interpret their cohabiting relationship as on the track toward marriage than their boyfriends. Women are more likely to believe that if they can coax their live-in boyfriend into marriage, "marriage will change him, making him more committed."

Professor Rhoades laments, based on her long-term research, that the facts "do not suggest a strong basis for such a hope."[18] This sets a lot of women like Wilma up for a significant dose of disappointment. And that can be harmful in many emotional and practical ways.

Other scholars have found that very practical domestic factors empower this relational inertia. The great majority of couples explain that their moving in together was strongly motivated by financial reasons. One young woman explained that her experience was very common among her female peers: "[My boyfriend and I] spent the majority of our time together, but yet we were both paying rent at two separate places and it just made more sense for us to live together."

Couples may have very pragmatic reasons for moving in together, but a marriagelike relationship needs to rest on a foundation that's stronger than just "saving on the rent." As the couple moves in together, they become financially dependent upon one another to maintain even the most basic financial life they have developed together.

This may be why cohabiting women are more likely than married women to be employed outside the home, even while cohabiting men consistently make more money than cohabiting women. And while cohabiting women are legally less protected in the breakup of their relationship than married women who get a divorce, cohabiting women often feel more compelled to stick with a less than satisfying relationship for their own financial security.[19]

SOMEONE trying to build

a case for how or why cohabiting favors

women would be hard-pressed to find

any evidence for their argument.

In turn this leads to the relational inertia that can suck both men and women into unsatisfying relationships. But it is different for women. When comparing men's and women's difficulties in ending a cohabiting relationship, "the perceived difficulty of terminating the relationship was strongest for women."[20] As we just learned, many of these women believe that converting the live-in relationship to a marriage might serve to "fix up" their partner into a better, more protective, caring, and providing sort of man. But these women learn—as the researchers have—that this turns out to be more wishful thinking than happy reality.

And because far more cohabiting relationships (as well as marriages preceded by cohabitation) break up than noncohabiting marriages, this implies that the cohabiting relationships that do stay together are themselves much less satisfying—particularly for the woman. In fact, someone trying to build a case for *how* or *why* cohabiting relationships favor women would be hard-pressed to find any evidence for their argument.

Ladies, if all this is not enough to give you serious second thoughts about settling for cohabitation, consider this last point that your feminist predecessors also got exactly wrong: Rather than being a more egalitarian relationship scheme where men are more likely to don an apron or become acquainted with a vacuum cleaner or toilet brush, just the opposite is true. A 2010 study finds what earlier studies found: Few cohabitors start their relationships with a fair balance between their bringing home the bacon, cooking it, then caring for and cleaning the house. And as the relationship goes on, this imbalance tends to get worse.[21] Guess which partner ends up picking up the larger share of the domestic duties? I'll give you three guesses!

Pamela Smock, working from the University of Michigan's Institute for Social Research, explains the bottom line women must consider:

> For their part, men may perceive or experience cohabitation as more advantageous than marriage. Given that cohabitation is typically more gender egalitarian in terms of labor force involvement than marriage, the arrangement relieves men of primary breadwinning responsibilities, while still providing them with domestic support; studies show that, even in cohabiting unions, women perform the majority of domestic work.[22]

Millions of women have been cohabiting over the past several decades. But this new informal institution has not even come close to improving women's relational and domestic happiness. In fact, any way you look at the data and the stories of the majority of cohabitors, women in such relationships have seen a substantial decline in their domestic happiness.

THE RELATIONSHIP
ON THE WOMAN'S TERMS

The feminist scripts on abortion, sexual openness, and cohabitation have not served womanhood well. And it is the smart young woman who learns from her older sisters who learned the hard way from their well-intentioned but ill-conceived ideas.

Marriage represents the relationship on the woman's terms because it favors the distinct nature of the woman. If you take the basic natures of both men and women across cultures and time, you find that sexual and relational standards that encourage commitment tend to favor the nature of women. Sexual and relational standards that diminish commitment tend to favor the man.[23] We have seen this demonstrated in various ways in the research and observations we've examined. We see it in the findings of anthropologists studying the sexual natures of men and women across diverse cultures. George Gilder explained this truth concisely and powerfully in his book *Men and Marriage*. He writes:

> In virtually every known society, sex is regarded either as a grant by the women to the man, or as an object of male seizure. . . . Managing the sexual nature of a healthy society, women impose the disciplines, make the choices, and summon the male efforts that support it. . . . Women domesticate and civilize male nature.[24]

Gilder continues with a powerful conclusion:

> The essential pattern [of male and female domestic and sexual relationships] is clear. Women manipulate male sexual desire in order to teach men the long-term cycle of female sexuality and biology on which civilization is based. When a man learns, his view of the woman as an object of his own sexuality succumbs to an image of her as the bearer of a richer and more extended eroticism and as the keeper of the portals of social immortality. She becomes a way to lend continuity and meaning to his limited erotic compulsion.[25]

She makes him become a better man. She does this because she is a woman. And she does this by having her man tie himself to marriage—a durable, clear relationship where the level of commitment is high and publicly understood, supported, and appreciated. She does this because she has the civilized role of humanity inscribed on the deepest fabric of her being. She does this through demanding the man commit all he has to her. If not, he gains no access to her intimacy—physical or otherwise.

And she has been doing it for millennia, wherever monogamy is society's rule. When monogamy is not the rule—either in polygamous or in sexually unrestrained cultures—women become objects to be collected and used by men. You can see it for yourself in these cultures. And we have heard it in dramatic detail from the women's voices in this chapter describing the fallout from the hookup culture.

Marriage defines the relationship on the woman's terms. And as such, it has the power to improve the lives of both men and women. This is *reality*—not antiquated ideology of some empty traditionalism—but demonstrable, scientific fact proved time and time again in the lives of millions of men, women, and their children. We ignore it at our own risk.

QUESTIONS
for Couples

1. Do you think that cohabitation has been more widely understood as something beneficial for women, harmful for women, or neutral?

2. Does it surprise you that men and women have differing expectations for where their cohabiting relationship is headed? Why or why not?

3. What do a man's and a woman's differing expectations mean for the future of the relationship? How likely do you think it is that either one's expectations will work out?

4. Besides the reasons mentioned in this chapter, what are ways that marriage could be the relationship that favors the woman's needs and cohabitation the relationship that favors the man's?

5. How do you see that *relational inertia*—sliding rather than deliberate deciding—could draw couples into cohabiting relationships and then draw those in unsatisfying cohabiting relationships into marriage?

RECOMMENDED RESOURCES

Scott M. Stanley, Sarah W. Whitton, and Howard J. Markman, "Maybe I Do: Interpersonal Commitment and Premarital or Nonmarital Cohabitation," *Journal of Family Issues* 25 (2004): 496–519.

Scott M. Stanley, Galena Kline Rhoades, and Howard J. Markman, "Sliding versus Deciding: Inertia and the Premarital Cohabitation Effect," *Family Relations* 55 (2006): 499–509.

Galena Kline Rhoades, Scott M. Stanley, and Howard J. Markman, "Pre-engagement Cohabitation and Gender Asymmetry in Marital Commitment," *Journal of Family Psychology* 20 (2006): 553–60.

Scott M. Stanley and Galena K. Rhoades, "Sliding vs. Deciding: Understanding a Mystery," *Family Focus on Cohabitation*, National Council of Family Relations, summer 2009.

Professor Scott Stanley's blog on marriage, cohabiting, and romantic relationships: http://www.slidingvsdeciding.blogspot.com/

Pamela Smock et al., "Heterosexual Cohabitation in the United States: Motives for Living Together among Young Men and Women," *Research Report 06-606*, Population Studies Center (University of Michigan, Institute for Social Research, 2006): 1–35. http://www.psc.isr.umich.edu/pubs/pdf/rr06-606.pdf

NOTES

1. Carter Heyward, "Abortion: A Moral Choice," *Frontiers: A Journal of Women Studies*, vol. 9, no. 1 (1986): 42–45.

2. "More Americans 'Pro-Life' than 'Pro-Choice' for First Time," *Gallup Organization*, Princeton, NJ, May 15, 2009; "Issue Ranks Lower on the Agenda: Support for Abortion Slips," *Results from the 2009 Annual Religion and Public Life Survey* (Pew Research Center for the People & the Press, October 2009), 5–6.

3. Miriam Grossman, M.D., *Unprotected: A Campus Psychiatrist Reveals How Political Correctness in Her Profession Endangers Every Student* (New York: Sentinal, 2006), xxi.

4. Laura Sessions Stepp, *Unhooked: How Young Women Pursue Sex, Delay Love and Lose at Both* (New York: Riverhead Books, 2007), 243, 255.

5. Stepp, 2007, 243.

6. Stepp, 2007, 35.

7. Conversation with Donna Freitas, May 15, 2009.

8. Donna Freitas, *Sex & the Soul* (Oxford: Oxford University Press, 2008), 9.

9. Pamela Smock et al., "Heterosexual Cohabitation in the United States: Motives for Living Together among Young Men and Women," *Research Report 06–606*, Population Studies Center (University of Michigan, Institute for Social Research, 2006), 14.

10. Galena K. Rhoades, Scott M. Stanley, and Howard J. Markman, "A Longitudinal Investigation of Commitment Dynamics in Cohabiting Relationships," *Journal of Family Issues* (in press, 2011): 22.

11. Smock et al., 2006, 5; Susan L. Brown, "Union Transitions among Cohabitors: The Significance of Relationship Assessments and Expectations," *Journal of Marriage and Family* 62 (2000): 833–46.

12. Hannah Seligson, *A Little Bit Married: How to Know When It's Time to Walk Down the Aisle or Out the Door* (Philadelphia: De Capo Press, 2010), 113.

13. Scott M. Stanley, Sarah W. Whitton, and Howard J. Markman, "Maybe I Do: Interpersonal Commitment and Premarital or Nonmarital Cohabitation," *Journal of Family Issues* 25 (2004): 496–519.

14. Galena H. Kline, Scott M. Stanley, Howard J. Markman et al., "Timing Is Everything: Pre-Engagement Cohabitation and Increased Risk for Poor Marital Outcomes," *Journal of Family Psychology* 18 (2004): 311–18.

15. Kline et al., 2004, 316.

16. Scott M. Stanley, Galena Kline Rhoades, and Howard J. Markman, "Sliding versus Deciding: Inertia and the Premarital Cohabitation Effect," *Family Relations* 55 (2006): 499–509.

17. Scott M. Stanley and Galena K. Rhoades, "Sliding vs. Deciding: Understanding a Mystery," *Family Focus on Cohabitation*, National Council of Family Relations, summer 2009, F2.

18. Galena Kline Rhoades, Scott M. Stanley, and Howard J. Markman, "Pre-engagement Cohabitation and Gender Asymmetry in Marital Commitment," *Journal of Family Psychology* 20 (2006): 553–60.

19. Smock, 2006, 6, 15.

20. Rhoades, 2011, 20.

21. Amanda Miller and Sharon Sassler, "Stability and Change in the Division of Labor among Cohabiting Couples," *Sociological Forum* 25 (2010): 677–702.

22. Smock, 2006, 6.

23. Paul Okami and Todd K. Shakelford, "Human Sex Differences in Sexual Psychology and Behavior," *Annual Review of Sex Research* 12 (2001): 186–241; Emily A. Stone, Aaron T. Goetz, and Todd K. Shakelford, "Sex Differences and Similarities in Preferred Mating Arrangements," *Sexualities, Evolution and Gender* 7 (2005): 269–76.

24. George Gilder, *Men and Marriage* (Gretna, LA: Pelican Publishing, 1986), 12.

25. Gilder, 1986, 13.

WE have been fused in our *marriage, in the commitment we have made to one another, in giving of ourselves totally and completely to one another. God has honored that in making us one flesh. It is true, beautiful, and deeply mysterious.*

8

LEARNING FROM THE BOOK OF SCRIPTURE AND THE BOOK OF SCIENCE

ONE THING YOU HAVE NOT SEEN in this Christian book on cohabitation is much mention of Scripture, save for some important information in the second chapter about how God put the desire for meaningful relationships so deeply in each of our hearts. We all long for relationships where we can be loved in beautiful and meaningful ways—and love another in the same way.

All cultures, regardless of their religion, politics, or laws have some form of marriage. Why do we find this? Because God put this desire for meaningful, long-term, and exclusive relationships into our basic human wiring. And as we learned at the end of the previous chapter, all cultures need the unique qualities of women to socialize the unique energies of men.

It is similar to water. God gave it to us, but He also put the desire and need for water deep within every person. Just as no individual can long survive without water, so also no culture can long survive without marriage. Like water to the human body, marriage is a basic element to evey society.

It applies to all humans as a common grace.

I have chosen to make the case that cohabitation is not a wise or healthy choice based not on Scripture but on science. You might ask why, as a Christian writer and student of the family, I have relied on science. Am I denying my faith? Some Christians might say I have. But they would be wrong, very wrong . . . with a shortsighted view of God. Let me explain!

If we understand how God and His world operates, we know that making such a strong distinction between the book of Scripture and the book of science is not being faithful to what we as Christians believe. God is the author and creator of all reality. He is therefore the author of both books, and He makes both available for to us to learn from.

Hymn writer Maltbie Babcock, a faithful Presbyterian pastor and lover of God's world, taught us to sing one of the church's great hymns, "This Is My Father's World." It is told that Babcock would take daily breaks from his pastoral duties and walk in the forest and rolling hills near his church. As he left, he would tell his secretary, "I'm going out to see my Father's world."[1] He could say this because he had the eyes to see the world for what it is.

His most famous hymn reminds us that the world—everything around us—reveals God's glory and His law:

> This is my Father's world,
> and to my listening ears
> all nature sings, and round me rings
> the music of the spheres.
> This is my Father's world,
> he shines in all that's fair;
> in the rustling grass I hear him pass;
> he speaks to me everywhere.

This is our Father's world . . . and *all nature sings, and round you rings the music of the spheres.* God has made reality in such a way that the universe can speak to us. Its revelation, which can't be held back, can teach us a great deal about itself—and about God! It not only speaks to us, *it sings.* And does so with a beautiful, powerful voice.

This is our Father's world . . . and *in the rustling grass you can hear him pass; he speaks to you everywhere.* Everywhere! There is no part of creation that cannot instruct us about God and His hand in it. This is our Father's world. We can listen to its instruction, and it points us to God.

But only if you have ears to hear.

God speaks to us through the Scriptures. It is His divine revelation. This is clear, for it is God's *Word*. But He also speaks to us through the *world*, His natural revelation. God's own Word tells us as much. Here are just two examples:

> Psalm 24:1–2
>> The earth is the Lord's, and everything in it,
>> the world, and all who live in it;
>> for he founded it on the seas
>> and established it upon the waters.

> Psalm 47:2
>> How awesome is the Lord Most High,
>> the great King over all the earth!

As a Christian writer trying to remain faithful, I can draw primarily from science in this book because God speaks to us through His creation—through our careful observations, measurements, and analysis of how humanity and His world works. This is the book of science, and it is open to the Christian. We don't have to choose between faith or science. For the Christian who understands this is our Father's world, it is *both/and*, not *either/or*.

Let's look quickly at how faith and science are not fundamentally at odds but rather how one produced the other.

SCIENCE FOUNDED ON CHRISTIANITY

The Christians of the late Middle Ages and the early scientists shared and were motivated by a Christian view of the world. It is well established that modern science was made possible because Christians understood the universe as our Father's world, believing it worked in an orderly fashion in accord with His design and laws—rather than at the capricious hands of the pagan gods who must be constantly appeased.

And they believed that we can observe, study, and, to a great degree, know God's laws of design. Rodney Stark, a sociologist and historian of religion, has written on Christianity's influence, for good and for bad, upon modern culture. He explains in his book *The Victory of Reason*:

> The so-called Scientific Revolution of the sixteenth century has been misunderstood by those wishing to assert an inherent conflict between religion and science. Some wonderful things were achieved in this era, but they were not produced by an eruption of secular thinking.[2]

Quite the opposite! In his earlier book *For the Glory of God*, Stark strikes at the popular, but false, dichotomy between faith and science. "Contrary to the received wisdom," he writes, "religion and science not only were compatible; they were inseparable."[3] He explains how this was so:

> The rise of science was not an extension of classical learning. It was a natural outgrowth of Christian doctrine: nature exists because it was created by God. In order to love and honor God, it is necessary to fully appreciate the wonders of his handiwork. Because God is perfect, his handiwork functions in accord with *immutable principles*. But with the full use of our God-given powers of reason and observation, it ought to be possible to discover these principles. These were the crucial ideas that explain why science arose in Christian Europe and nowhere else.[4]

And this is exactly what we have been doing in this book. Being faithful by seeing how God's immutable principles for intimate and domestic relationships are illuminated through the ever-expanding pages of the book of science. And we have learned some important, powerful, and persuasive truths.

GOD'S immutable principles

for intimate and domestic relationships

are illuminated through the

pages of the book of science.

This is what I find time and time again as one who seeks as a Christian to research the truths of marital, family, and sexual relationships. I discover constantly that rather than contradicting God's Word, well-done, honest science—free from advocacy and political or ideological influence—supports what God tells us is best for us.

And this is precisely what we have discovered in these pages regarding cohabitation and marriage. The book of science gives witness to the book of Scripture. And why shouldn't it? Both have the same author.

GOD'S HEART ON MARRIAGE

We have looked at the science. Now let's look at the Scripture.
Where is marriage in God's story? What is His heart on the matter?
It doesn't take us long in reading His Word to get an answer. You find it in the first book of the Bible.

When God created man and woman, He did not set them up as business owners, founders of a church, teachers, artists, cooks, sports figures, or even as carefree singles. The moment man and woman appear on the earth, God acts as the officiator of their wedding. At God's choosing, the first activity between God, man, and woman is a marriage.

Think about that a moment. It says something about God's view of marriage, doesn't it? As we saw in chapter 2 of this book, the only time Adam and Eve were unmarried, God had something profound to say about it. Adam is created, but single. Eve is not yet there—still just a wonderful idea in God's mind.

God said of this situation, "It is not good for the man to be alone" (Genesis 2:18). Something in God's perfect creation was not as it was meant to be. God solved this fundamental problem in a dramatic way. He gave Adam a wife. And He gave Eve a husband. Not a buddy, a sidekick, a business partner, or someone to hang with and fix his dinner. God gave him a spouse.

Quiz question: What are the first words of humanity recorded in Scripture? They are Adam's words about his *wife*! We find them in Genesis 2:23:

> This is now bone of my bones
> and flesh of my flesh;
> she shall be called "woman,"
> for she was taken out of man.

Adam notes that she is like him in her humanity, but also very different. She is a woman! He can't miss it. He notes her feminine form. He is like any other guy. And guess what? God doesn't scold him for his carnality but delights in Adam's excitement over her. This is what man was made for—and what woman was made for. They are made for each other, physically, emotionally, domestically, soulfully, intellectually, creatively.

And God oversees their wedding as His first action with them. Before Adam and Eve become anything else, they become husband and wife. And God delighted in them. It was His will.

And then, in the next verse after Adam's exclamation, God tells us something else very important about this man and woman. About what they have become as husband and wife. Genesis 2:24 says:

> For this reason a man will leave his
> father and mother and be united to his
> wife, and they will become one flesh.

Let's look at what is being said here.

> . . . a man will *leave* his father and mother . . .

This implies a husband forsakes all other relationships that were once important to him—even his most essential ones with his own parents. His wife is now where his allegiances lie. There are no other contenders. She is it.

. . . and be united to his wife . . .

The King James Version uses the word *cleave*, while the English Standard Version uses *hold fast.* God would have us think of a tight, close relationship that is permanent—not superficial or transitory. I prefer the word *cleave.* It puts in our minds the image of a very intentional and strong hanging onto, as does *hold fast.*

But cohabitation is neither a *leaving* nor a *cleaving.* Instead, it is keeping our options open. And so it is not God's best for us, not what He created us for. Should we be surprised it doesn't work out as well?

But God's description of this new union, this marriage, is boldly dramatic:

. . . and they will become one flesh.

Two distinct beings—one male and one female—become something they were not . . . *one flesh.* Remarkable!

This is both figurative and literal. Figurative, in that I am one flesh with my wife, Jacqueline. But she is home in Colorado, and as I write this I am in the back bayou country of Louisiana. But it is literal as well, because we really are one flesh. It is neither just sentimental nor symbolic.

We have been fused in our marriage, in the commitment we have made to one another in giving ourselves totally and completely to one another—and God has honored that in making us one flesh. It is both true and beautiful.

One of C. S. Lewis's friends, Charles Williams, once wrote that while sex outside of marriage was bad morals, divorce was bad metaphysics.[5] In that curious statement, he underscored this one-flesh nature of marriage. Separating two people who are one flesh is as impossible metaphysically as cubing a sphere.

Jesus also taught this view of marriage. Some religious leaders tried to catch Jesus in a trap, so they asked Him about marriage. Jesus asked these men if they didn't recall what God said "at the beginning." He then quoted the truth of Genesis to them—reaffirming this fundamental truth from Genesis 2:24. Read Jesus' words for yourself in Matthew 19:4–6.

Jesus is pointing His listeners—the religious leaders of His day and now us—to this *leave, cleave,* and *one-flesh* nature of what sexual, domestic, and parenting relationships between men and women should look like. Both cohabitation and what that is often likely to produce—divorce—do not reflect God's best for any of us.

This leaving and cleaving, the giving of ourselves totally—emotionally, willfully, physically, sexually, financially—to our spouse, holding *nothing* back, is the gift we owe our most beloved. This is what God intends, for it's what delights Him and is therefore what is good for us. Both the book of Scripture and the book of science demonstrate this.

WHY GOD MAKES RULES

It's important for us to know that God holds marriage as His ideal, not because He picked some things at random to put in the "Thou Shalt" column and some others in the "Thou Shalt Not" column to make our lives miserable. On the contrary, God directs our behaviors and decisions for two primary reasons:

> One, they honor Him.
> Two, they are what's best for us.

Honor God, and He blesses that. All the research we have observed in this book testifies to that reality. Think about that! God wants us to cleave to our spouse, denying all others. Giving all of ourselves and holding nothing back.

When we make that kind of commitment in marriage—rather than holding back in cohabitation—what does science say happens to us? It has taken a whole book to explain all the ways God blesses it. Whether the sociologists and other researchers realize it, this is the story they are helping to tell. They are showing us how God's world works. (But let's not tell them they are God's preachers.)

We should also note that we don't find marriage only in the first chapters of Genesis. We also find it in the last chapters of the Bible. God's book starts with a marriage and ends with a marriage—but a marriage of a very different kind.

In Revelation 19:7–8, we read:

> Let us rejoice and be glad
> and give him glory!
> For the wedding of the Lamb has come,
> and his bride has made herself ready.
> Fine linen, bright and clean,
> was given her to wear.

This concluding wedding is not a ceremony between a man and a woman but is the great culmination of history—the great and glorious wedding feast enjoyed between the Lord Jesus Christ and His bride, who has been made ready for Him. The bride of Christ is the church. And He has been seeking her throughout the history of the world.

God is seeking each of us to be there at His great wedding, as part of His bride. His unending and unquenchable love for us—for you and for me—compels Him to seek us, to woo us, to win us, to have us respond with our yes to His proposal of love, fidelity, care, and betrothal. This is what God's story is all about. And rather than getting down on one knee to propose to us, He put His only Son on a cross as a dramatic wedding proposal. On this cross, He covered our sins so we could wear white to His wedding. (See Isaiah 1:18.)

And we all have a role to play in that story, by accepting His proposal or telling Him no.

What will your answer be?

The New Testament teaches the nature of God's proposal to us in Revelation and also in Ephesians. There the apostle Paul brings up the verse we have been studying, given to us by God the Father in Genesis and by Jesus in Matthew 19. Paul says in Ephesians 5:31:

> For this reason a man will leave his father
> and mother and be united to his wife,
> and the two will become one flesh.

He continues in verse 32:

> This is a profound mystery—but I am
> talking about Christ and the church.

The apostle Paul makes a clear, unmistakable connection between the earthly marriage of Adam and Eve and all men and women who say yes to the glorious betrothal between Jesus—the Creator, King, and Ruler of all creation—and His beloved bride, the church, made up of all true believers throughout history who have freely given themselves to Him without reservation—all their heart, soul, and mind—holding nothing back. And you can be a part of that!

Marriage holds nothing back. Cohabitation, by definition, does. Marriage is a huge deal to God, for you can't read His Word and draw any other conclusion.

Don't settle for anything less than God's best.

QUESTIONS
for Couples

1. If this is our Father's world, what are some of the ways God communicates to us in two important books: the book of Scripture and the book of science?

2. How can we strengthen our faith by looking at how these two books complement one another?

3. Do you find it interesting to find a connection between what God says about relationships and what science is recently discovering? What points are most significant to you and why?

4. While the Bible may not speak of cohabitation specifically, where and how does Scripture give us insight into whether cohabitation fits God's plans for our relationships?

RECOMMENDED RESOURCES

Mike Mason, *The Mystery of Marriage* (Colorado Springs: Multnomah, 2005).

Gary Thomas, *Sacred Marriage* (Grand Rapids: Zondervan, 2000).

NOTES

1. Kenneth W. Osbeck, *101 Hymn Stories* (Grand Rapids: Kregal, 1982), 272.

2. Rodney Stark, *The Victory of Reason: How Christianity Led to Freedom, Capitalism and Western Successes* (New York: Random House, 2005), 12.

3. Rodney Stark, *For the Glory of God: How Monotheism Led to Reformations, Science, Witch-Hunts and the End of Slavery* (Princeton, NJ: Princeton University Press, 2003), 3.

4. Stark, 2005, 22–23.

5. Charles Williams, *The Forgiveness of Sins* (Grand Rapids: Eerdmans, 1942), 117.

MARRIAGE tends

to produce more happiness in our lives

than any other adult relationship.

The reason for this is the unique

nature of marriage—the commitment

and self-sacrifice it demands.

9

MARRIAGE IS
MORE THAN . . .

Aʟʟ RELATIONSHIP FORMS are not created equal.

Cohabitation is not a junior, apprentice form of marriage.
Cohabitation is not an on-ramp to marriage.
Cohabitation is not marriage's spring training.
Cohabitation is not marriage-lite.

Cohabitation is just "moving in together" so we can save some money on rent, spend more time together, and see how the relationship works out.

Marriage is an action, a decision, a statement.

Marriage is giving our all to another and stepping up and proclaiming it to the community of people around us. And that commitment makes us different kinds of people, different partners, different parents. It says we are clearly for another, or at least that's what the others around us—those who witnessed our exchange of vows—expect of us. Marriage demands something of us. And this expectation makes us act differently.

Marriage is definitive. Marriage is absolute. Marriage leads us into new worlds—and it closes off others.

This is the virtue of marriage. This is why marriage makes real, measurable differences in our lives, as we have seen in the previous pages.

Marriage is so much more than we tend to think it is.

MARRIAGE IS MORE THAN THE WEDDING

Too many young couples today act as if the wedding is what marriage is primarily about, rather than just simply the doors a couple passes through on their way into matrimony. Researchers and journalists who talk to young couples about why they are delaying their marriage find these couples often explain they aren't marrying because they can't yet afford a wedding.

To listen to these young folks, mostly the women, one would think their pastor or the clerk at City Hall will reject their application for a marriage license because they can't spend at least $10K on their wedding.

When Jackie and I got married in 1982, big weddings were as much the craze as they are today. But we were two kids who had fallen in love in high school and wanted to get married as soon as we could. Our wedding probably cost $800, including rings, Jackie's dress, and my dorky white tux. No one told us we were dishonoring marriage.

We were, however, honored by the number of people who told us that night and afterward that it was one of the most beautiful weddings they had ever attended. It certainly wasn't because we put on an impressive party on such a tight budget. It was because our wedding was the simple, honest celebration of the commitment two young people were making to one another. Today, we would describe it as "organic." Then, we just didn't have much money. Less was more. It had to be. There is absolutely no research showing that couples who drop a gigantic wad on a wedding bash have longer, happier marriages than those who don't. In fact, those who think the ceremony is the big thing probably end up less satisfied in their marriages. They are focused on the frosting rather than the cake. Those who invest themselves in the marriage that comes after the wedding are investing in something that really matters. And it will pay serious dividends in the form of contentment, intimacy, support, love, and genuine happiness.

I saw a billboard on the interstate some years ago with an important message:

"Loved the wedding! Now, invite Me to the marriage!"—God

It's a good message for all couples planning their wedding.

MARRIAGE IS MORE THAN GETTING A SOUL MATE

I am not a fan of the soul mate concept of marriage. You see this idea in commercials for certain online dating services. "We will help you find the spouse of your dreams with our super-duper matching system," they claim. Do I think they should help you find the match of your *nightmares*? No. But this "I want to marry my soul mate" idea of marriage gets it wrong on two important levels.

First, marriage is not like a shopping trip where we scan the aisles looking for that perfect *something* we need to complete some need in our life. A spouse is not a consumer product we shop for to fulfill us in just the right way.

Second, marriage is not so much about us and our needs and wishes. The soul mate idea of marriage makes it about us—and turns our spouse into something that suits us, for us. And when this person reveals their human flaws to us in the intimate microscope of marriage, we become prone to wonder if this imperfect person is really the God-given soul mate we thought we were getting. It happened with the first two humans. And it has happened with most couples since.

So should husbands and wives not be soul mates? It is not a question of *whether* but *when*! Find any couple successfully married thirty years or more and ask about their spouse as their soul mate. Then ask if their spouse was their soul mate from day one. They will most likely laugh. You see, we don't marry our soul mate. *We marry the person whose soul mate we want to become.* And the key word is *become*. The soul mate status of a relationship usually takes time—sometimes a great deal of time. And only after many bumps in the road. Marriage doesn't *give* a soul mate, it *makes* a soul mate: out of us—and out of our spouse. And these soul mates are the best kind.

MARRIAGE IS MORE THAN "HAPPILY EVER AFTER"

Where have you heard the line "and they lived happily ever after"? It's not announced by the pastor as the newly married couple walks down the aisle. We hear it only in fairy tales.

Did I just throw a big cup of cold water in someone's face about happiness and marriage? Not at all! We've seen in these pages that married people tend to be happier on a wide scale of measurements—more so than people who are single, dating, cohabiting, or divorced. Married people enjoy very high levels of happiness. But they don't enjoy *constant* happiness.

Marriage has its struggles, hardships, and heartaches. Again, find any couple married thirty-plus years and ask if they have lived "happily ever after." If you ask my wife and me (we've been married *almost* thirty years), we would look at each other with knowing smiles and answer, "For the most part!" But our marriage, like all marriages, has gone through some very difficult times.

MARRIAGE is a joy,

but it is also hard work.

This is one of its strengths.

Marriage is a joy, but it is also hard work. This is one of its strengths. As one man told me about his own marriage, "There are days I feel I could trade my wife for a warm diet Coke; but those are rare. Most days she is the greatest thing going!"

These less-than-happily-ever-after days make us better people—and make the good days more fulfilling. This is one of the reasons marriage makes us better people: It compels us to hang in there through the rough times and see it through. To try to do better next time.

Marriage can be compared to wise retirement investing. Pick a good stock. Stick with it through the highs and lows. Make substantial, regular, and occasionally even painful contributions to it over a lifetime. You will find over time that you have a greater treasure than you could have imagined.

MARRIAGE IS MORE THAN ABOUT YOU

As we have seen, marriage tends to produce more happiness in our lives than any other adult relationship. There is a reason for this. It has to do with the unique nature of marriage—the commitment it demands.

Happiness is never a destination we can run straight toward. We can't pursue it directly. In fact, those who put a great deal of energy into seeking happiness are the ones less likely to find it. The happiest people are typically busy doing other things. And marriage is a strong route to happiness because in marriage we gain the opportunity—even the privilege—to live for and serve others. This means first and foremost our spouse, then our spouse's extended family as they enter our life and we learn to love them, and then our children.

Marriage increases our happiness because marriage is more likely than any other relationship to make us live for others. Marriage keeps doing this in my life. And those who know me best know that I too often fail. It makes me struggle. It makes me work harder to be more giving. But this work also makes me happier. Marriage has this effect on most of us.

The first chapters of Genesis teach us that the first two humans became husband and wife before they became anything else. This was God's plan—and delight—for them.

Marriage builds a relationship like no other. It makes a difference. And that difference is very good.

Marriage is more. Don't settle for less.

QUESTIONS
for Couples

1. What aspects of marriage do you imagine cause it to provide more happiness, health, and longevity than cohabiting?

2. Why might a big wedding contribute to a happy marriage?

3. How could a big wedding tend to distract from the importance of the marriage itself?

4. Why do you think happiness is not a destination you can run directly toward? How are you more likely to get there by pursuing other routes?

5. Ask four couples who have been married thirty years if they started out as soul mates, or if they became soul mates over time. Write down what you learn from these couples and discuss how this can strengthen your own relationship.

RECOMMENDED RESOURCES

Scott Stanley, *The Power of Commitment* (San Francisco: Jossey-Bass, 2005).

Les and Leslie Parrott, *Saving Your Marriage Before It Starts* (Grand Rapids: Zondervan, 2006).

Les and Leslie Parrott, *Saving Your Marriage Before It Starts, Workbook, for Men, for Women* (Grand Rapids: Zondervan, 2006).

Willard Harley, *His Needs, Her Needs* (Grand Rapids: Revell, 2011).

ACKNOWLEDGMENTS

This is a book written with the wonderful benefit of a full month off from my day job so that I could concentrate on just a few things: eat and shower once in a while, luxuriate in my big pile of collected research studies, and write out the text of this book. Being able to work like this is nearly every writer's dream. Many weeks of ready-to-expire vacation time, my generous brother Todd, his wife and their kids who let me occupy their guest room, and the librarians at my two alma-maters—Pensacola State College and the University of West Florida—all made this project possible and productive. Oh yes . . . and my incredible wife, Jacqueline, and our five kiddos played no small part, willingly (or eagerly?) doing without me for a few weeks.

During this sabbatical, I was also able to take nearly a week away from my writing to head up deep into the swamps of Cajun country and spend a remarkably rich time of spiritual retreat, reflection, and renewal. This was at the Parish Hermitage, run by Dr. Eddie Parish and his gifted wife, Judy, in St. Amant, Louisiana. If you are looking for an especially rich experience of honest spiritual direction, amazing food, quiet, beautiful surroundings and no phone or television, the Parish Hermitage is your place. Yes, this is a commercial!

Also, I thank the many scholars I refer to in these pages. So many of them have been kind and brilliant teachers to me over the years through their writing and valuable friendships.

And in the long hours of research and writing, I always have friends who sit and keep me company via iPod. The soundtrack for this project was thanks to Leonard Cohen, the Raconteurs, Lucinda Williams, Patti Smith, Suzanne Vega, and Jenny Lewis.